I'm on the Internet, Now What?!™

by Matt Lake

justme.com

SILVER
LINING
BOOKS
NEW YORK

For information contact:
Silver Lining Books
122 Fifth Avenue
New York, NY 10011

First Edition
This edition was published by Silver Lining Books.

Printed and Bound in the United States of America

Other titles in the Now What?!™ series:

introduction

"I finally got a computer so I could get on the Internet," sighed Patricia McCluskey, "but it seems I have to get a Service Provider, something called a browser, and then I can get an e-mail address. Why does it all have to be so complicated?"

It doesn't have to be. That's why we came up with *I'm on the Internet, Now What?!* It has all you need to know, from getting connected to learning how to surf the Web. There's no jargon, no confusing techno-speak, no strange diagrams. Just the basics, pure and simple, and in English. You'll learn how easy it is to find a Service Provider and use your browser like a pro. Not to mention the inside track on how to shop, research, and make travel arrangements all online. In short, we give you all you need to know to really use the Internet.

We promise painless understanding and tips that you can put to use right away. So start reading. The information highway is calling you.

Barb Chintz
Editorial Director, the Now What?!™ Series

table of contents

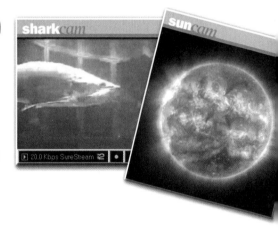

CHAPTER 1 LOGGING ON

THERE'S A WHOLE NEW WORLD OF
COMMUNICATION, ENTERTAINMENT, AND
INFORMATION OUT THERE IN THE ONLINE
WORLD. SO FIRE UP YOUR COMPUTER,
STRAP ON YOUR VIRTUAL SAFETY BELT,
AND GET READY FOR THE RIDE OF YOUR
LIFE. NEXT STOP . . . THE INTERNET.

LOGGING ON

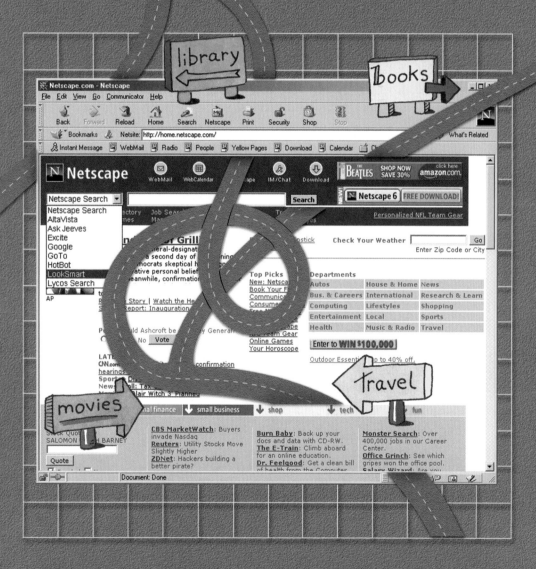

all about the Internet

The Internet is a huge computer network that's best explained by its nickname, the Information Superhighway. Think of it as a giant highway that wraps around the world, with bazillions of little byways and dirt tracks connected to main streets and huge freeways. Instead of cars and trucks, the traffic on the Internet is little packets of computer information. Some of these packets contain text only, such as electronic mail (or **e-mail**) messages, while others are elaborate packets full of pictures, text, even sounds. These babies are called **Web** pages.

Web pages can also contain **links** (called hyperlinks —more on those later) to other Web pages. It's these links that give the World Wide Web its name. If you could see a join-the-dots game between all the Web pages on the Internet, you'd see a pattern of threads as intricate as a spider's web.

So where's the on-ramp to this webby highway? Look no further than an **Internet Service Provider** (or ISP to its friends) to get you online. In most cities and towns, you can choose from many ISPs—whether from the phone or cable company, or a dedicated Internet company like America Online.

ASK THE EXPERTS

Where did the Internet come from?

We have the Cold War to thank for the Internet. Back in the 1950s, the U.S. Department of Defense funded computing departments at universities, which created **supercomputers** (huge computers that the D of D needed to plan military strategy quickly). A little later, in the 1960s, the D of D had another project—to develop a communications network that could withstand heavy bombing. What they came up with was a computer network that hooked up universities and military supercomputers. Universities across the world used the network to share information and research. Since then, millions of commercial networks (such as AOL) have joined up with these supercomputers—and things have never been the same.

Is the Internet the same thing as the Web?

No, it's not. The World Wide Web (or the **Web** to its friends) uses the Internet to deliver its Web pages and sounds and pictures. But if the Internet is the highway system, then the Web has destinations on that highway. In fact, Web pages aren't even the most popular use of the Internet. Every year since it started in the 1960s, the Internet roadway has delivered more pieces of electronic mail (e-mail) than any other kind of information.

getting connected

Drive your
computer to the
Internet—by phone

So the Internet's like a huge road and your Internet Service Provider is the on-ramp. Great, you're good to go. But wait. Before you can get connected to the Internet, your computer needs a piece of equipment called a **modem**. Almost every computer you can buy these days contains a piece of hardware called a modem that's designed to plug into your phone wall outlet. The phone outlet, you ask? Yes, the Internet travels via the phone line. (It also travels via cable lines. More on that on page 12).

To make sure your computer has a modem installed, take a peek at the back of it. You'll see a lot of sockets (computer people call them **ports**) of various shapes and sizes. If you see two ports side by side that look like the phone socket that you'd plug your phone into, you've got a modem.

Now you need only a bit of phone wire long enough to reach from a phone wall outlet to the back of your computer. Plug one end into your phone wall socket (the jack) and the other into your modem port. Wait, hang on, some computers have two modem ports. Make sure you don't use the one that's labeled PHONE or has a picture of a telephone. (That port is for an extra telephone line.) You want the one that says LINE or has a picture of a modem above it.

When your modem is ready to roll, you're all set to hook up with a service provider. But first you need to know how fast your modem runs. Most **modem speeds** these days are rated at 56,000 bits per second (sometimes called 56K). Some older ones top out at 33,600 bits per second or 33.6K. When you come to select a dial-up number with your service provider, these numbers will be important. If you just got a new computer, just assume its modem runs at 56K.

STEP BY STEP: SETTING UP YOUR MODEM

1. Click on Start, then Settings, then select Control Panel.

2. Double-click on the Modems icon (symbol) in Control Panel.

3. If your computer has a modem, you'll see its name. To find out its speed and other settings, right-click on the modem's name, and select Properties.

4. If you don't see a modem installed, you need to install one. Click the Add button and follow the instructions in the Install New Modem wizard.

EXTERNAL MODEMS

If your computer doesn't have a modem built in, you can get one from most electronics and office stores. The easiest type to add is what computer types call an **external modem**. These sit outside your computer, so you don't have to mess around unscrewing your computer's casing and installing circuit boards. These little boxes are about the size of a paperback book, have their own power cord, and connect to the back of your computer with what computer folks call a serial cable. This plugs into your computer's serial port, a socket about an inch wide with 15 little holes in it—known to its friends as a COM port.(If your computer has two serial ports, you want the smaller one.) Once it's plugged into your computer, into the phone jack, and into the power supply, you'll be equipped to get online. Don't worry . . . it'll be worth all the effort.

broadband connection

If you want a fast connection to the Internet, get broadband

Before you make the final jump onto the Internet, there are two much faster ways to get your computer onto the Internet. One uses your TV cable line to transfer Internet information, and the other uses a souped-up phone line. Computer folks call these faster connections **broadband.** Think of them as wide multilane highways compared to the narrow "dirt track" of a 56K modem connection. In fact, these connections are quite a bit faster—cable Internet can top 1,500,000 bits per second or 1550K. That's more than 25 times as fast as a regular 56K connection.

If you subscribe to cable television, check with your cable company to see if they offer Internet access. Many do, and if they don't, maybe other cable operators in your area do. If you can't use television cable to get online, look into a **DSL** (digital subscriber line) connection. DSL uses your phone lines to get connections four or five times as fast as a regular modem. And better still, neither hogs your phone while you're online, so you can hold conversations on the same phone line that's connecting your computer to the Internet. Naturally, you pay more for cable Internet and DSL than if you used your regular old phone line. Most people wet their feet on regular phone lines before plunging into the high-tech speed of broadband.

An external broadband modem (left) is required equipment and is supplied by either your phone or cable company.

ASK THE EXPERTS

How easy is it to set up a cable Internet connection?

Usually someone from either your Internet Service Provider or your TV cable company comes to your house to do it (easy) or you are given a kit to do it yourself (not easy). This is how it works:

1. Plug your computer into a special cable modem they provide—a boxy thing a little bigger than a paperback book.

2. If your computer doesn't contain a **network card** (also called an ethernet card) that connects your computer to other computer networks, namely the Internet), you need to install one and connect that to the cable modem.

3. Connect your new cable modem to the nearest cable outlet.

4. Program your computer's settings so it knows how to communicate with the service provider.

Network Card

How do I get DSL, the souped up phone-line connection?

To find out who's providing DSL connections in your area, look in the phone book under Internet. Also, call your local phone company and see if they are in the business yet. Once you find a service provider who does DSL, they'll supply you with a special external DSL modem to plug into your phone line. Chances are you'll need a new phone line for it. You'll then need to plug the DSL modem into a network card in your computer and follow the specific instructions from your service provider for setting up your software.

How much does cable-Internet connection or DSL cost?

Your regular old slow phone line Internet connection costs now about $20. Costs vary for cable and DSL connections, but it's typically $30 to $40 a month (for more on payment, see page 23). And there may be a onetime installation and setup cost too—up to $100—so keep your eyes open for special setup deals before you leap in.

getting your Mac online

The ads
didn't lie—
it really is easy

Your Mac is a different animal from other personal computers. It was designed to be easy to get online—and it really does live up to its promise. We'll take you through the steps you need to perform to configure your computer. (That's computer-speak for typing in phone numbers and codes and clicking on stuff—no screwdrivers necessary!) Probably the hardest step is to get a length of phone line with a plastic plug at either end and slot it into the back of your Mac or iMac and into the phone jack in the wall. And that's only difficult because you may not be able to see the back of your computer to ensure that you get the plug in the right way up. (A hint: the little clip that stands out of the plug should be at the top of the plug).

Once you've connected the wires, setting up the computer is pretty straightforward. Many people leap straight onto the

Internet when they set up their Mac for the first time. When you first run your iMac, for example, it will show a video of how to use the mouse, then ask you to register your computer. The third setup step asks, "Do you want to get on the Internet?" To sign up right then and there, click on either the free trial access button (to take advantage of Apple's Internet access service) or "I'll use my existing Internet service" if you've signed up with another ISP.

Of course, these steps aren't available to you if you haven't signed up for the Internet. But have no worries—look for an Internet icon (symbol) on your desktop. One click on this, and the Mac Internet Setup Assistant will open. Otherwise, go the Apple icon and look for the Internet folder. Click to open it.

You'll need some information from your service provider before you proceed:

1. The provider's name and Internet phone number

2. Your user ID and password

3. Some technical mumbo jumbo: the default and secondary DNS IP addresses. These two long numbers seem intimidating, but think of them as phone numbers that Internet computers need, and they won't seem so bad.

4. Your e-mail address and password

5. The e-mail server names (two names, which may be called POP and SMTP servers). Don't let the terminology throw you—think of them as letter boxes and post offices that your computer goes in order to deliver and pick up mail.

With this info, you have all you need. Start up the Internet Setup Assistant. Click on Yes in the Internet Setup Assistant windows when it asks, "Would you like to set up your Mac to use the Internet?" After that, you'll see a new screen with the question "Do you already have an Internet account?" Assuming you've already signed up with an ISP, you click on Yes and fill out information on ten or so different screens. Your service provider will give you all the information you need.

And at the end of this process, you click the Go Ahead button and your Mac will dial up the Internet.

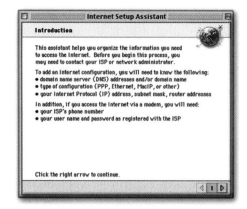

iMacs have an Internet Setup Assistant folder to help you with all the steps to connect.

shopping for Internet Service Providers

They're the phone companies of the Internet world— and they're not monopolies

An Internet Service Provider is like a phone company—you need its services to connect to cyberspace, the brave new digital world out there. And it's like your phone company in another way too— it's not a monopoly. There are hundreds of Internet service providers (or ISPs as they are called in Netland), ranging from big national and international companies to smaller local ones that provide service for only a couple of towns. All an ISP needs to operate is at least one **server** (a powerful computer) and a connection to the Internet, which they in turn share with you for a small monthly fee. All your computer has to do is dial into the ISP's server and when it picks up, bingo! you're online.

All ISPs also provide you with an **e-mail** (electronic mail) box, along with software to send messages from your computer and pick up incoming messages from the Internet. (See Chapter 2 for more about e-mail). Many also give you room on their Internet server computers to put up your own Web pages. (More on that in Chapter 8.)

There's another kind of ISP—it's called an **online service.** The main online services are America Online (AOL), the Microsoft Network (MSN), and CompuServe. These services give you access to private Web pages and other services that only their online subscribers can see. It's a bit like a large Internet club.

Whether you go with an ISP or an online service, the fees are pretty much the same: a flat fee of $15 to $25 a month. But as with the phone company, there are several different types of accounts, tailored for different usage patterns. Some ISPs, for example, charge a much smaller fee for service, but charge for your connection time by the hour.

Before you sign up with an ISP, you will need to think up a user name for yourself. This might be your last name or a nickname. Whatever name you do pick, remember that it will be part of your e-mail address—so you may regret any choice that's too cutesy or hard to type. Oh, and have a couple of alternatives on hand, since it's possible that your first choice may be taken.

Most ISPs let you have more than one e-mail address. To protect your privacy, it's a good idea to also register for an e-mail address using a name no one could trace to you. Use your real name e-mail address for family and friends; use the anonymous one for the Internet public at large.

SHOP AROUND FOR AN ISP

To find good deals on ISPs that operate in your area, borrow someone else's Internet computer (or use a public access Internet computer at your public library). Check out these two sites.

CNET Web services   http://webservices.cnet.com

Don't know where to start looking for an Internet Service Provider? CNET does a great job of getting you started. Its services range from articles in its Help Center to large regional listings of dial-up, DSL, and cable modem providers. It's a good idea to shop around for Internet service, and CNET provides a big list which you can sort in order of cost. But its list of ISPs is shorter in some areas than those in our next favorite ISP resource. . .

The List   http://thelist.internet.com

The List may be exaggerating a little by calling itself the Definitive ISP Buyer's Guide, but it's not far wrong. Its listings aren't as convenient as CNET's—they're sorted by area code, which makes it hard to figure out which is cheapest—but there are thousands of services listed.

signing up with ISPs

The Internet awaits you

Great, you've found an ISP that suits your needs. Now what? You need to register online. Gulp. Don't panic. It's not difficult, but you do need to pay attention to make sure you get everything right the first time. Take a deep breath and make sure you have these vital elements close at hand: your computer hooked up to the Internet, a working telephone, a pen and paper, and your credit card. If you are going with an online service, turn to page 20.

MAKING THE CALL TO THE ISP

1. First, call up your prospective ISP. Tell them the service plan you want (dial-up monthly unlimited, monthly limited hours, or whatever). Tell them how you'll be paying (credit card, check). And tell them the user name you want (see page 17).

2. They will give you two key pieces of information to write down:
   a Internet phone numbers that your computer can dial. (If they're really geeky, they'll call the number a POP, a telephony term that's short for point of presence.)
   b Next write down their Internet address—which they may call a DNS, or IP. It'll be a series of numbers grouped into four clusters, for example: 198.83.19.241. (Chances are you won't need to input these numbers, but write them down just in case.)

3. They'll give you a password to use (which you'll probably be able to change later to something you'll remember). Some ISPs may let you pick your own password right from the start.

4. Great. You are now officially connected. The next step is to tell your computer how to find this new connection.

STEP BY STEP: SETTING UP AN ISP ACCOUNT

1. Click on Start, Programs, Accessories, Communications, and click on the Dial-Up Networking icon.

2. Double-click on the Make New Connection icon.

3. Across three screens in the Make New Connection wizard, enter a name for your connection (your ISP's name is a good choice) and the access phone number from your ISP. Click Finish.

4. An icon for your new connection will appear in the Dial-Up Networking folder. Right-click on it, and select Properties.

5. Click on the Networking or Server Types tab or button (it has a different name depending on which version of Windows you're running).

6. Make sure that the drop-down list box labeled Type of Dial-Up Server is showing PPP: Internet.

7. Now click on the TCP/IP Settings button. If your ISP gave you one Internet address, click on Specify an IP address and enter it there. If you have two, click on Specify name server addresses and enter them there.

8. When finished, click the OK button in each dialog box to exit.

9. When you first click on your connection to get online, you'll need to enter your user name and password.

using online services

Going with the big guys
Want to get online but don't want the hassles of fiddling with your Windows network settings? That's one of the reasons that online services are so popular. Online services like America Online, the Microsoft Network, and CompuServe use their own sign-up software to bypass much of the tedium of setting up your account. Most home computers come with online sign-up software already installed. If not, chances are you've gotten a few free sign-up software CDs in the mail from the big online providers.

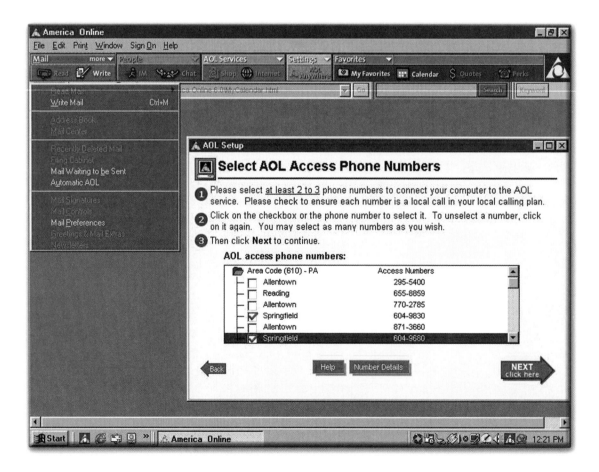

STEP BY STEP: SETTING UP AN ONLINE ACCOUNT

1. Check that your computer came with the online sign-up software you need. Turn on your computer and make sure your modem is plugged into the phone line. Click on Start, Programs, Online Services, and pick a service from the list.

2. If your computer doesn't have that program you want, try calling your online service provider and ordering the software from them. (See the phone numbers at right.)

3. Select the new member option.

4. Enter your telephone area code. The program will then check its list of local access numbers and make a few suggestions for numbers your computer may dial to get onto the Net. Be careful when you make your selection—make sure you pick a number that's near where you live and doesn't carry any connection charges from your phone company. Pick two or more numbers; that way, if the first number your computer dials is busy, the online service software will just dial a back-up number. Simple!

5. You then need to enter your personal details and credit card information. If you don't have a credit card, America Online can take its payments directly from your checking account, in which case you'll need to copy some numbers from the bottom of your check.

ISP versus online

Should you go with a plain, no-frills local ISP, or a fancy-schmancy online service? What to do? First, of all don't fret, it's not as hard as it seems. In the end, the decision comes down to which gives you the best experience—and that boils down to three things.

- Do you often have to wait to get online?

- Do they often drop the online connection while you're online?

- Do they provide good customer service?

The first two issues are often dependent on where you live. A service provider could have fewer customers in one area than another, and so there are fewer busy signals. Also, the connection could be fast in one area but slow elsewhere. If it takes more than 5 minutes to get online, that's too long.

Customer service is key. You'll often get better personal service from a medium-sized local ISP than from an online giant like America Online. If you call a local company for help, they'll know the state of your local phone network better, and they tend to go the extra mile for their customers. You'll often find much better price deals with them too—where AOL and big national companies charge $21.95 a month, you can probably get unlimited access from a local company for $19.95, $14.95 or even less a month.

That said, America Online, Microsoft Network, and bigger national service providers such as Earthlink have more resources to guide you through your online time. America Online's channels of information—news, entertainment and so on—are so easy to use that even **newbies** (a slang term for Internet beginners) can use them. And online services also have a lot of unique content that most Web surfers have a harder time getting at—including chat rooms, chat events with celebrities, and copyrighted articles and pictures.

ASK THE EXPERTS

How exactly am I billed for Internet service?

Different companies bill in different ways. If you get Internet access through your phone or cable company, the service charge will be another line item in your monthly phone or cable bill. Most other companies require a credit card on which they charge your monthly or annual fee. Some companies will let you pay by check—they'll send you an invoice, and you send them a check. You can often get a few bucks off your monthly fee by paying three to six months in advance, or by the year.

What's the best deal for online service?

In fact, the competition for your business is so great in most areas that a lot of service providers will give you a free trial for a month before they start charging your credit card. Use this time to see whether you like their services. Pay particular attention to whether you can get online when you want to—or whether the number is always busy when your computer tries to dial in.

FIRST PERSON DISASTER STORY

The bargain that keeps on charging

Twenty-one dollars a month seemed like too much to pay for the Internet. So when I saw a local ISP offering service for $10 for "light use," I jumped on it. I wasn't planning on using the Internet that much—a little e-mail and some stock trading, that's all. So $10 for 10 hours a month seemed just right.

My plan was to do forty minutes every few days reading and writing my e-mail. It was going to be close, but I figured that I'd make it in under the wire—and besides, if I spent an extra hour online, they only charged $2.50 per hour for overtime. I'd still only be paying $12.50 a month instead of $21.

Boy, was I wrong. It turned out I'd spent 14 hours and 21 minutes online. My bill was $22.50. I should have realized I wasn't going to have the discipline to watch the clock. I'm on the unlimited monthly plan now.

Cindy M., Montgomery, Alabama

surfin' by browser

If you want to write a letter, you need to run a word processing program. But if you want to explore the sites on the World Wide Web, you need to use a Web **browser**—software that lets you move around the Web. There are many browsing programs, but the most popular are Microsoft Internet Explorer, Netscape Navigator, and those browsers that come with America Online and CompuServe's software. How do you get Web browser software? You probably have one or two in your hard drive waiting to be launched. Otherwise, your Internet Service Provider will mail you at least one (on a CD-ROM) when you sign up.

STEP BY STEP: LAUNCHING YOUR WEB SOFTWARE

1. Find the name of your browser under the Start menu's Programs option and click on it. Often, the browser's icon (small picture) may be on your Windows desktop, where it's much easier to load.

2. When the browser opens, it will usually connect you to the Internet right away. If not, you may see a dialog box called Dial-Up Connection— you just click the Connect button.

3. The first page you'll see is the **home page** of the browser. To go to a different Web page, you can type a Web address (such as **www.yahoo.com**) into the Netsite or Address box at the top, and press Enter.

4. Get familiar with your browser's navigation buttons. Here's what they do: **Back** returns you to the previous page, **Forward** takes you ahead one page. Use **Reload** or **Refresh** when your browser gives up before a page is fully loaded. **Home** takes you to the first page you see when you start your browser. **Search** takes you to a Web search site. **Print** prints the page you're at. **Stop** is what you hit when a page is taking forever to load, and you're not that interested anyway.

HAT IF

You found a really interesting site, but you clicked past it and can't remember where it is?

Happens all the time. That's why every browser has a history list—a kind of electronic trail that helps you to find your way back. To see the last few sites you've visited, click on the little down arrow by your browser's Back button, and a drop-down list will appear. You can also click the down arrow next to your Web address or Netsite field—the one that shows the address of the Web page you're looking at right now. If this cool site was something you saw yesterday or last week, check the long-term history list—in Internet Explorer, hit the History button; in Netscape, there is no button, so you'll need to hold down the Ctrl key and press H.

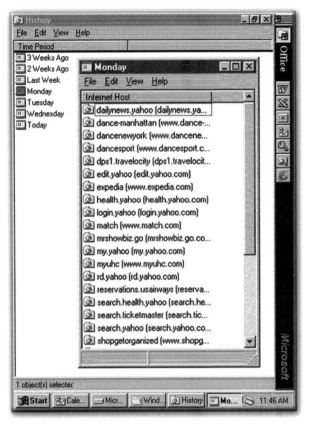

You see a blank box with an X in it instead of a picture?

Web pages sometimes fail to deliver pictures because the site is temporarily too busy. Right-click on any blank picture. In the drop-down list that appears, click on the Show Picture option.

A Web page takes a long time to appear?

Some Web pages are packed with graphics and those just take time to download onto your computer.

Netscape *at a glance*

When you first load your Netscape browser, don't let the mess of little pictures, different-colored text, and other clutter get to you. Here's a quick guide to the World Wide Web as seen through the Netscape browser. If you're using another browser, turn to the pages for Internet Explorer and the America Online and CompuServe browsers.

B

A Navigation toolbar: These buttons help with the most common browsing tasks—for details, see page 24.

B Bookmarks button: Everytime you find a new Web site you can bookmark it by clicking the Bookmark button and choosing Add Bookmark. It will save it to your list of favorite websites for easy access.

C Netsite or Address field: Here's where you type in Web addresses to visit.

D What's related: If you like the site you're at, click this button for a list of similar sites.

E List box: Whenever you see a box with a down arrow at the right, click for a list.

F Text box: Click in here to type in something you want to find and then. . .

G Enter button: Click here to search for what you've typed in at F.

H Link: Click on a link to jump to another Web page. Text links are easy to spot— they're underlined and colored blue.

27

Internet Explorer
at a glance

The browser that's built into Windows is called Internet Explorer, and it's been part of every version of Windows since 1995. Don't be put off by all the bells and whistles—it's pretty easy to figure out. Here are the basics, all laid out for you.

A   Navigation toolbar: these buttons help with the most common browsing tasks—for details, see page 24.

B   Favorites button: Do you like the page your at? Click here to save it to your list of favorite Web sites.

C   Address field: Here's where you type in Web addresses to visit.

D   Search window: When you click the search button, this side panel appears.

E   List box: Whenever you see a box with a down arrow at the right, click for a list.

F   Text box: Click in here to type in something and then . . .

G   Enter button: Click here to get the results.

H   Link: Click on a link to jump to another Web page. Text links are easy to spot—they're usually blue and underlined.

built-in browsers
at a glance

Online services like America Online and CompuServe have their own Web browsers built in. This means that they look and act a bit differently from regular browsers. But don't fret! The differences are minor. And inside AOL or CompuServe software, you'll see plenty of other little windows in addition to the home page. Once you get the hang of that, you're off and running.

A Navigation tools: These buttons help with the most common browsing tasks.

B Address field: Here's where you type in Web addresses to visit. It also works for AOL keywords.

C Internet button: When you click this button, the browser window (E) opens.

D Welcome window: This isn't actually part of a Web browser, though it looks like it. It gives information that AOL thinks will interest you.

E Browser window: Okay, this is part of the Internet. All the rest is part of the online service's software.

F Link: Click on a link to jump to another Web page. Text links are easy to spot—they're usually blue and underlined.

G Favorite places button: Like the page you're at? Click here to save it to your list of favorite places. And get to know the other buttons at the top right of each window—the flat line shrinks screens down to reduce clutter.

now what do I do?
Answers to common questions

I typed in a Web address right, but I still see a message saying it doesn't exist.

Don't panic. Popular Web sites often get busy, and post such messages—its way of turning around and saying "Not now, I'm busy!" Don't take this for an answer! Click on the Refresh or Reload button on your Web browser's button bar. If still nothing, try again the next day. If there is still nothing, then the site has been removed from the Web.

Some Web sites don't end in .com. Why?

Techies call the bit at the end of a Web address a top-level domain, and .com is only one of dozens of them. Of course, it's the most popular one on the Web, hence the slang word dotcom for any Web-based company, but many others exist. Two of the most popular are .net and .org, which are theoretically earmarked for networks and nonprofit organizations. But in practice, anyone can register a .com, .net, or .org address. (You can too—as you'll see in Chapter 8). Here are some other top-level domains you'll see:

.edu – a university or educational foundation
.gov – a government Web site
.us – a site in the U.S. (includes the state, as in .ny.us)
.co.uk - the U.K. equivalent of .com

When I try to go online, I get a busy signal. What should I do?

This happens for various reasons. Could be your ISP or online server is too busy to take your call and get you online. Or it could mean a problem with your phone line. The best solution is to keep trying. If you don't connect after 10 minutes, pick up the phone and call the customer support line. They should be able to provide some help.

What is a dead link?

It's not nearly as gruesome as it sounds. . . but it's not much fun either. Here's the story: You're at a Web site and you see a great sounding link, so you click on it. The next thing you see is. . . nothing. A blank page with the words This Page Not Found. Dead links are common in Web sites put together by amateurs—sometimes people don't double-check that they've typed in the link properly when they made their Web page. And sometimes, Web pages are taken away and any links to them at other pages automatically become dead links.

I love AOL's service, but I miss Internet Explorer as my browser. Can I use both?

Yes. Here's a little-known trick that lets you use AOL (or CompuServe or MSN) to provide your online connection, while your other Internet software does the actual surfing. First, connect to your online service. Now open your other browser (in Windows, click the Start button and look under Programs for your browser name). Bingo! up pops a browser that can use the Internet like a pro.

I want to change my service provider and sign up with a new one. How do I do that and not lose any e-mail?

You old service provider will not forward any e-mail. If you change your e-mail address, you need to contact all your computer correspondents and let them know your new address. This is why people are reluctant to change service providers.

OW WHERE DO I GO?!

CONTACTS	PUBLICATIONS
Yahoo Internet Life http://www.yil.com	**Internet and** **World Wide Web Simplified** IDG Books
Internet for Beginners http://netforbeginners.about.com	
Focus on AOL http://aol.about.com	**Sams Teach Yourself the** **Internet in 10 mintues** By Galen Grimes
	America Online for Dummies By John Kaufeld

CHAPTER 2 E-MAIL

ONCE YOU'VE USED E-MAIL, YOU'LL WONDER
HOW YOU LIVED WITHOUT IT. YOU CAN SEND
A MESSAGE ONLINE TO ANYWHERE IN THE
WORLD AND IT'S THERE IN AN INSTANT.
MOREOVER, IT'S CHEAPER THAN A PHONE CALL,
AND FASTER THAN PAPER MAIL. NO WONDER
IT'S THE MOST POPULAR THING TO DO ON
THE INTERNET.

E-MAIL

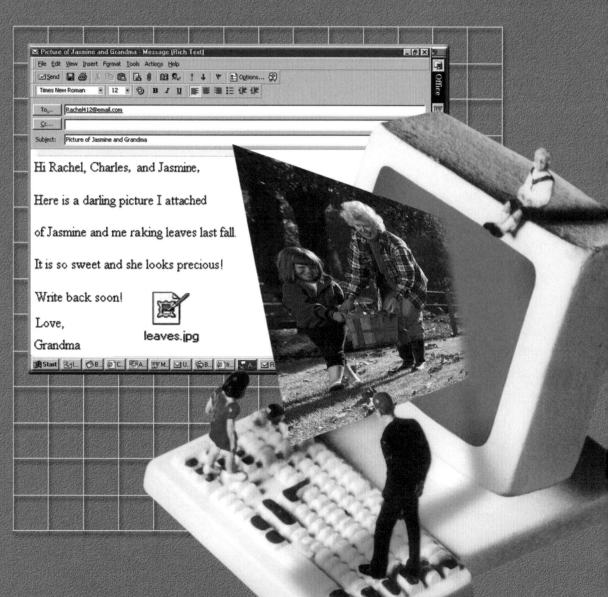

e-mail software

Electronic mail (e-mail for short) is the single most popular use of the Internet—and it's easy to see why. You can send an unlimited number of messages without licking envelopes, buying stamps, or trudging out to the mailbox in the rain. And most impressive of all: your e-mail greetings can reach friends in less than a minute—no matter where in the world they are. Also, unlike telephone calls, e-mails never interrupt people in the middle of dinner.

Like everything to do with computers, e-mail needs software. But don't worry—it comes with your **browser** software, which tells your computer how to get on the Internet (see page 24). Usually, e-mail software has its own name. In the browser program Internet Explorer, the e-mail program is called Outlook Express. Netscape Messenger is the e-mail software name for the Netscape browser. And America Online has its own built-in e-mail software, which just goes by AOL. Another popular e-mail program is Microsoft's Outlook. Your Internet Service Provider, (see page 18), may give you different software free. Eudora and Pegasus are two popular examples.)

Sometimes you need to go through one extra step to tell your e-mail software its exact settings. Good news: it isn't necessary for America Online or other online services that use their own special e-mail software. Your Internet Service Provider will give you the necessary information.

In Netscape Messenger, you
1. Click on Edit menu
2. Select Preferences, and click on Mail Servers
3. Type in the mail server names for incoming and outgoing mail
4. Click OK.

In Outlook Express, you
1. Click on Tools
2. Select Accounts, click on Add, and select Mail
3. When a Wizard dialog box pops up, enter the mail servers' names
4. Click OK.

 **ASK THE EXPERTS**

Where does e-mail go?

While you're typing your e-mail, it's on your computer screen and nobody else can see it but you. When you hit the Send button, it whizzes across the Internet to a **server** (a big computer) at your service provider, called an e-mail server. Like a post office sorting room, your service provider's e-mail server figures out where the mail needs to go and sends it there. Within minutes, the message ends up in the recipient's ISP e-mail server, where it is held until the recipient goes online and picks it up.

Is e-mail private?

No, it's not. Think of e-mail as a message written on a post-card—anybody could read it. If you mistype an address, a total stranger could get your message. (If there is an error in the address, your Internet provider will send you an automated message telling you it could not deliver your message.) If the recipient of your message gets his personal e-mail through his work, then the tech people at his company are legally allowed to read his messages. A word of caution: don't put anything too private into your messages.

you@email.com

Set up your own e-mail box

Ready to start your new life as an online letter writer? Great. It's easier than you think, because when you sign up with your Internet Service Provider, you automatically get at least one e-mail address. All you have to do is give your service provider a **user name,** kind of like a computer handle, that is special to you—for example, johndoe@msn.net or doeman@msn.net. (If that user name is taken, they will ask you to come up with another one.)

It's a good idea to take a moment and think of a good user name because it will become your e-mail address. This means that it should be something that identifies you (a name, nickname or hobby). You should also keep it short and simple. Why short? Remember that people have to type this in. Lots of letters will make this harder and could result in misaddressed mail. (Some online providers let you choose several user names, and each one comes with its own e-mail address.)

ASK THE EXPERTS

My service provider keeps rejecting my choices for user names for e-mail addresses. What do I do?

There are rules about what you can use in e-mail addresses. The Internet only allows letters, numbers, and three types of punctuation—a period, hyphen (-) and underscore (_). No other characters will work in an e-mail address. You can't use spaces either. And capital letters don't count—JoeBlow@aol.com and joeblow@AOL.com look the same to e-mail software. Sometimes you have to get creative!

What are the dots for?

As a global postal service, the Internet uses its own address system. Instead of a street address, city, and zip codes, the Internet uses **domains**—they're the familiar "dotcom" names in Web site and e-mail addresses. Like the address on an envelope, domains have a format—and they use periods (called dots) to separate the various elements. You'll sometimes see several dots in an address, usually in the business e-mail addresses in big corporations. So don't be surprised by something like betty.smith@admin.nowhere.com.

your first e-mail

Here's how to find it and read it

You've got an e-mail account, now what? You've already got mail! Every e-mail provider sends you a welcome message or two, just to get you started. You'll know you've got mail because your software will tell you—either using the sound of a voice proclaiming, "You've got mail," or some electronic beep or a blinking icon.

But where is that mail hiding, you ask? It's in your e-mail's inbox. (Think of it like a regular inbox on your desk—mail comes into it, you pick it up there and read it.) If you're using America Online or some other online service, click on the mailbox icon or one of the mail buttons at the top of the screen. For other e-mail programs, click on the Inbox listing at the left of the page.

Most e-mail software lists the unread items in bold or colored text so you can see at a glance what's new. The list should show the sender's e-mail address, the subject of the e-mail, and the date and time it was sent. To read a message, click on it. If a single click doesn't make the message appear, double-click instead, and that will do the trick. After you have opened and read the message, its listing will revert to normal type. Some e-mail programs automatically store it in your Old Mail or Read Mail folder, others just let it stay in your inbox indefinitely until you delete it.

Every time you turn on your computer and go online, you will automatically be notified about any new mail. Once you are online, most programs automatically check for new mail every 20 minutes.

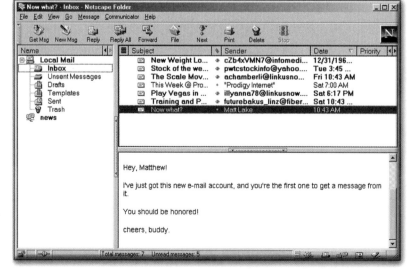

ASK THE EXPERTS

My inbox soon fills up with messages I've read. How can I delete them?

Old e-mail messages take up your computer's hard disk space. Delete the messages you don't want. You do this by clicking on the message in the Inbox to highlight it, then clicking the Delete button.

How can I delete mail without reading it?

Some e-mail programs are automatically set so that as soon as you click on a message it opens. If you don't want that **default,** or automatic setting, you need to change it. In Netscape, go to View in the tool bar and select Show. Click to remove the check mark from the option Message. In Outlook Express, go to View, select Customize Current View, and click on the link for Show Messages, to change how you want your messages viewed.

My e-mail in AOL keeps getting deleted. How do I stop that?

If you want to keep AOL messages once you've read them, click on the Keep as New button. If you don't, they'll disappear behind the Old Mail tab—and after a couple of days, vanish forever. The alternative is to save your AOL e-mail to a Filing Cabinet (that's AOL-speak for a folder on your hard disk). Here's how:

1. Click on the Settings menu, and select Preferences

2. Click the Filing Cabinet link.

3. Click to put a check mark in the boxes next to the two options Retain All Mail I Send in my Personal Filing Cabinet and Retain All Mail I Read in My Personal File Cabinet.

4. When you click on OK, these changes affect all your screen names at once. Bingo! you've got mail . . . permanently.

sending e-mail

Messages to the world...

You want to send a message to a friend, colleague, or company? They're only a few taps on your keyboard from knowing what's on your mind. How to start? The first thing you have to do is click on your e-mail software's Compose Mail or New Mail button. A new window will pop up. See opposite page for what all those boxes, also called **fields**, signify.

A Send To: Here's where you type the recipient's e-mail address (you can send to multiple addresses).

B Copy to: (Optional) Want to send to more than one person? Here's where you type other e-mail addresses, sometimes as many as 10. Some e-mail software also has a BCC field (which stands for blind carbon copy). This means the BCC e-mail recipient remains a secret to the others you are e-mailing to.

C Subject: All e-mail messages need a description—some software won't send e-mail without one. Make your subject short and descriptive so your recipient "gets" what it's about right away.

D Formatting tool bar: Not all e-mail programs let you format the text, but if they do, here's where you can change the style, size, and even color of your writing.

E Message window: Where you type your message. Click in this space and start typing. Here's a tip: Read back over a message before you send it, just to make sure, before you click on the Send button.

F Attachments button: If you want to send a picture or other computer file along with your e-mail message, click here. Some software uses a paper clip icon instead of using the word attachments.

G Send button: Done with your message? Send now or send later are the choices with America Online. With other software you just get "Send."

REPLY OR FORWARD

You can also reply to or forward a message you've received. With the message open, click on the button labeled Reply or Forward.

If you're replying, the Send To and Subject fields will be filled with the original sender's e-mail address and the original subject, prefaced with Re: (short for referring to).

If you're forwarding, you'll have the original message and subject in the message window and subject field—only the subject will have FW: (short for forwarded). Just start typing your message and it will appear along with the original message you received.

opening attachments

**There's a little some-
thing in your mail**

Wait, it gets even better. With e-mail you can also send (attach) all kinds of things with your messages, such as a computer file or a digital photograph, even a movie clip. (Yes, e-mail can handle a bit of video.)

You can always tell when new e-mail in your inbox has an attach-ment because it will have a paper clip or an arrow or something next to it to signify it's got an attachment. When you open the message, you'll see a file name somewhere, usually with a box around it.

Now what do you do with an attachment? Detach it (also know as **downloading**) so you can open it. Some e-mail programs let you open it directly while you are in your e-mail program or store it in a download folder for later; others require you to save it first to a place on your computer (your desktop or hard drive), and exit your e-mail program before you can read it.

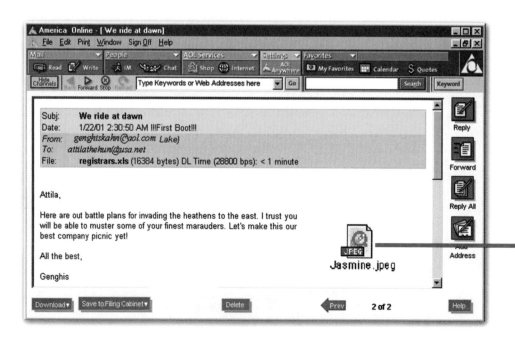

An attachment comes with clues about what it is. If it's a Microsoft Word document, it should have .doc at the end of its file name; an Excel spreadsheet will have .xls following its name. And it should open automatically so you can read it and even edit it and then save your edited version to your hard drive.

If it's a **compressed** file, it's a file that takes up so much memory it would take forever to download. How to tell if it's compressed? Compressed files usually have .zip or .sit at the end of their file name. Special software is needed to open these files.

viruses

An **e-mail virus** is a computer virus that is inserted into an e-mail attachment. Should you open the attachment, the virus is let out to create havoc with your computer. Some viruses are relatively harmless, but others can delete files or send out embarrassing e-mail messages.

How do you catch a virus? By opening an e-mail attachment that contains a virus. (You can't catch a virus just by clicking on an e-mail; it's the attachments that cause the trouble.) The good news is that you can spot most viruses by looking at the file name of the attachment. Don't open any attachment if the last three letters of the filename are .exe or .vbs—for example, homepage.html.vbs.

And if an e-mail from a stranger contains links to Web sites, don't click on them. Some (very few) Web sites can have viruses hidden in them. You won't come across such sites by regular Web surfing, but some malicious e-mailer could send you to one.

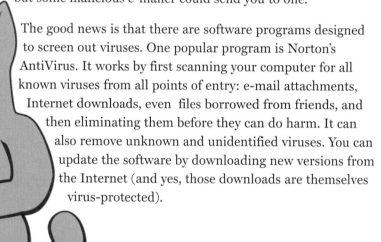

The good news is that there are software programs designed to screen out viruses. One popular program is Norton's AntiVirus. It works by first scanning your computer for all known viruses from all points of entry: e-mail attachments, Internet downloads, even files borrowed from friends, and then eliminating them before they can do harm. It can also remove unknown and unidentified viruses. You can update the software by downloading new versions from the Internet (and yes, those downloads are themselves virus-protected).

ⒶSK THE EXPERTS

**I just got sent an e-mail attach-
ment that looks like it's a virus. How
did the sender get my e-mail address?**

People who create these viruses (sometimes called
hackers) know how to get into directories of e-mail
addresses. But sometimes the sender is an unwitting
friend who opened an e-mail attachment that had a virus, only
to have the virus steal all the e-mail addresses in his computer
and send the attached virus on to them. If that's how it happened, don't be too hard on your friend.

**I keep getting e-mail notes from friends about such and
such a virus going around. Are they for real?**

No. The forwarding of e-mail warnings about viruses are
nearly always hoaxes. If you get a message warning you about
an impending virus, ignore it. Whatever you do, don't forward
it on to your family, friends, or coworkers.

Where can I buy virus protection software?

Most computer stores that sell software sell virus protection
software. It costs about $50.00.

sending attachments

Your computer's hard drive is probably a treasure chest of cool things—ranging from digital pictures of your pets to that first draft of the Great American Novel you've been working on. If you want to share any of the stuff you have there, then e-mail is a great way to do it.

And it's easy to do, too. When you're composing an e-mail message, check out the tool bar at the top of your software for a paper clip icon, or some other button labeled Attach or Attachment. Almost all e-mail software has one—even Web-based e-mail services such as HotMail and YahooMail.

STEP BY STEP: SENDING ATTACHMENTS

1. When you click on the Attach button, a dialog box appears.

2. Check out the drives on your hard disk, and click on the one that contains the file. (The drive labeled c: will be your hard disk, where most of your files are stored.)

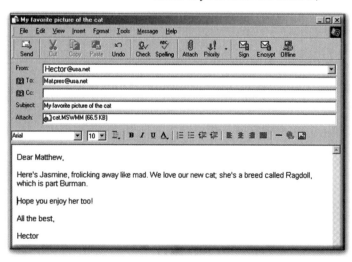

3. Look for the folder in which your file is stored (maybe My Documents or My Pictures, which you will find under the Windows folder if you can't see them anywhere else).

4. When you find the file you want to share, double-click on its icon (the little picture next to it). Click on OK if the dialog box is still open.

5. You'll be returned to the message you're writing, but you'll see a new element on the screen—the name and size of the file you just attached.

6. If the wrong file is listed, you probably misclicked in step 4. No problem—just right-click on the attachment, select Delete from the drop-down menu that appears, and start again.

That's all. When you send the e-mail, the attachment will go with it.

# ASK THE EXPERTS

Why does it take so long to send an e-mail attachment?

The bigger the attachment, the longer it takes to to send. And anything larger than 2 megabytes (about the size of two 8x10-inch digital photographs) won't go through at all. The smaller the attachment, the faster it goes to the sender.

I have to send a big file! What can I do?

Your only choice is to **compress** the file you have. If you have Windows '95, '98 or 2000, you will need to download a software program called WinZip (see pages 44, 69 for information about downloading). This program will both compress files for easy mailing and decompress them back to normal size for viewing. You can also buy it at your computer or office supply store.

To compress a file, you need first to select the file, then right-click on it (use the *right* button on the mouse). A menu bar will come down. Choose Add to Zip, then follow the WinZip directions. To open a compressed file, you simply double-click on it and drag it to your desktop, then double-click to open it. (It will uncompress on the way to your desktop.)

If you have Windows Millennium Edition (Windows ME to its friends), you have something like WinZip built in. To use it while you are in your e-mail program, click on the attachment paper-clip, and find the file you want to attach. Then use the *right* mouse button to click on it and select Send To. Click on the option Compressed Folder, and Windows will shrink the file down into what looks like a folder, but which is actually a file with the same name but with the extension .zip.

unwanted e-mail

Spam, spam, spam… and more spam

Your mailbox at home probably receives a lot of junk mail—unwanted advertising, pitches for magazine subscriptions, and low-rate preapproved credit card offers. Unfortunately, your e-mail inbox is likely to suffer the same fate. Sending e-mail is cheap for mass marketers, and so as soon as they get hold of an e-mail address, they will add it to their list and blast you with ads. In computerland, junk mail is called **spam**.

But spam doesn't end with unwanted ads. Many people use the word to describe any kind of unwanted e-mail—which includes jokes, chain letters, pornographic advertisements petitions, and virus alerts (hoax messages alerting you about an e-mail virus). Some people like getting jokes in their e-mail box, but all these other types of mass e-mail are universally disliked. Unsolicited messages from pornography Web sites are a nuisance as are chain letters. Virtually all virus alerts are completely bogus; and any petitions sent by e-mail are usually a scam by e-mail marketers to get fresh e-mail addresses to sell to their advertisers.

FIRST PERSON DISASTER STORY

A Dear John e-mail

I was upset with my boyfriend and decided to write him an e-mail telling him exactly what I thought of him. So I dashed off a message full of pretty robust language and strong accusations. And I sent it off to him—or at least that's what I thought. Next day at the office, people were acting weird around me, avoiding contact. Ours is a pretty friendly office so I wondered what was going on, and asked a friend. It turns out that I typed the wrong e-mail address into the box, and it went to a mailing list of people I work with instead of my boyfriend. I couldn't show my face around the office for a week, but I learned a lesson. Don't write e-mail in anger, and always check your address before sending.

Josie L, San Mateo, California

STEP BY STEP: DELETING SPAM

1. Stop spam at the source. E-mail marketers must get your e-mail address from somewhere. Make sure it's not from you. Don't give out your e-mail address to a business you don't want to do business with.

2. Get a special junk/spam e-mail box. If a Web site insists on having an e-mail address from you before it will let you in, create a special box and never check it. America Online lets you set up as many as seven user names. Make one specially to give out to people or Web sites that you don't want to hear from.

3. Be anonymous in chat rooms and forums. Use a special user name to go into chat rooms or post messages on Web forums. Make sure you don't give out your main e-mail address to anyone in a chat room until you trust them. There are even automatic software "monitors" that go into chat rooms to grab e-mail addresses for Internet mass marketers.

4. Turn on "spam filters." Some Internet Service Providers and most Web mailboxes keep a list of known junk e-mailers, and at your request will block any and all e-mail from those sources. Check in the Help menu for any reference to junk e-mail or spam for specific instructions.

5. Request removal. Many responsible direct e-mailers will provide the ability to unsubscribe from subscription e-mails. Check the end of any e-mail for unsubscribe instructions. But be careful—if the e-mail reads like a "get rich quick" scheme, the sender is probably running some kind of scam. Don't send your e-mail address or click on links in suspicious e-mail. That will just confirm your e-mail address and open the door to more unwanted messages.

your e-mail address book

Take a letter, computer

Instead of struggling with long e-mail addresses, you can use shorthand, thanks to your e-mail's electronic address book. This is a contact list that can store names, e-mail addresses, and even phone numbers and other details of your friends and family.

Before you can use your address book, you need to have names and addresses in it. As you get e-mail from friends who you want to include in your address book, you can add them one by one. Look for the button or menu option that lets you add a message's sender to your address book—check under the Tools menu or click on the Addresses or Address Book button. You can also do it in one sitting by taking your paper address book and typing in all your contacts with e-mail addresses at once. It's your choice.

This is a pretty typical e-mail list—it contains names in one column and full e-mail addresses in the next. Type in the name, the e-mail program fills in the address. Bingo!

To address e-mail using an address book, you simply open the book and double-click on the name from the list you want. In most software, you can just enter a shorthand name (such as "Bob") into the "To:" line, and your e-mail software will fill in the address for the Bob on your list. If there's more than one Bob, you'll get a list of Bobs to choose from. See, it's not so hard.

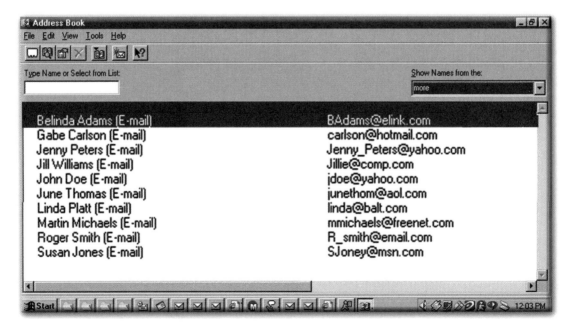

ASK THE EXPERTS

Can I edit the information in my address book?

Naturally! The steps vary slightly depending on your software, but it's basically very easy. Just open the address book and click to select the entry you want to edit. If your software shows an edit or properties button, click it and make the adjustments. If you don't see such a button, right-click or double-click on the entry until you see an option. When you've corrected the entry, click on OK, and the changes will be made.

Can I delete a name from an address book?

It couldn't be much easier. Open the address book, click on the name to select it, and press the delete key on your keyboard. The e-mail software will ask if you're sure—it's easy to click on the wrong name—so you must click Yes to finish the process. Poof! The contact vanishes.

I'd like to include my name, title and favorite Web page at the end of every e-mail. Must I type it every time?

Not at all. All you need do is create a signature, or sig, and apply it to all your outgoing mail. The exact steps vary depending on the software you use. In Outlook Express, for example, click on the Tools menu, select Options, and click on the tab marked Signatures. Click the New button, and type in what you'd like at the end of every message. Then click the box labeled Add Signatures to all outgoing messages, and finish off by clicking OK.

When I sent an e-mail to my friend I got a message back that said "Mail System Error." What happened?

Most mail servers (the post offices of the Internet) will let the sender know if there's a problem delivering mail—but they use scary terms like "fatal error" and "system error." It usually means that your message can't be delivered, usually because the address is wrong. Check the address again and resend the message.

lists and groups

E-mail isn't just a one-on-one thing

Great. You're now an e-mail pro. So much so that you are now sending out e-mails to a slew of people. Chances are, you are copying friends and family on some of your e-mails and you're getting tired of typing in half a dozen e-mail addresses in the Copy To box.

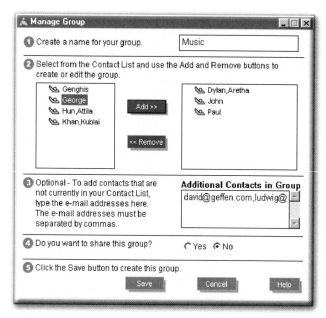

Stress not—let e-mail lists come to the rescue! E-mail lists and groups are just what they sound like—a collection of e-mail addresses that have something in common. And the hardest thing about making them is figuring out which e-mail addresses you want to lump together. Once you've decided on that, your course is easy; check out the steps on the opposite page.

Your personal e-mail group lists function like a holiday card list; you manage the addresses, and handle all the mailings. All the members of the group can see the e-mail addresses of the other members in the Send To Box. If they select Reply To All when they respond, they'll be able to send a message to all the other people on the list.

Creating your very own e-mail list is as easy as picking names from a list. In America Online's software, you pick names from your address book and click the Add button. Ta-daa! You're done.

Group e-mail is such a valuable tool that newsletter publishers, big-time companies, and special-interest groups use it to handle large-scale publication and broadcasting. When things reach a large scale, there's a need for more controls—such as hiding subscriber e-mail addresses and handling requests to unsubscribe. For this reason, newsletter publications turn to **list servers**—Web companies that automate large-scale mailing.

STEP BY STEP: CREATING A GROUP

Setting up an e-mail group is easy as pie. These instructions are tailored to America Online's software, but all e-mail programs work in a very similar way.

1. In the Mail menu on the toolbar, click on Address Book.

2. In the Address Book window, click on New Group to create a new group list

3. In the Manage Group window, enter a name for the group.

4. Click on names in your contact list, then click the Add button to add them to your group.

5. If you have addresses not currently in your contact list, type them afterwards.

6. Click on Save.

7. In your address book, you'll see a new entry in bold text. It's your new group.

EDIT THE GROUP

Some people may ask to be removed from your list, and maybe some others want to be added. Don't worry—your group listing can be edited. Here's how.

1. In the Mail menu on the toolbar, click on Address Book.

2. In the Address Book window, click on the name of the group to edit. It will be in bold letters.

3. In the Manage Group window, click any name that must be removed in the right window; click the Remove button. To add other names, click their names in the left pane; click the Add button.

4. Click on Save.

now what do I do?

Answers to common questions

I'm seeing a lot of acronyms in e-mail. What's BTW? Who's TIA?

E-mail is a bit like the old-time telegraph—people try to keep things short and to the point. Sometimes they overdo it! Here is a list of some of the more common acronyms people use in e-mail and chat.

BFN – bye for now	BTW – by the way
FWIW – for what it's worth	FYI – for your information
IMHO – in my humble opinion	IMO – in my opinion
LOL – laughing out loud	ROTF – rolling on the floor (laughing)
TIA – thanks in advance	TTYL – talk to you later

I got an e-mail message that is full of color graphics, asking me to click on a link. What's up with that?

You have received a Web page. They can contain pictures, cool text effects, and Web-style links. Most e-mail software can handle mail that's written in **HTML** (hypertext markup language), the code that's used for Web pages. When you click on the link, your browser will show a Web page. If this e-mail comes from a friend or a company you trust, click on the link and check out the page. But if you don't know who sent the mail, don't click the link, and delete the message right away. Some Web pages may contain viruses that can damage your computer.

I deleted mail from my HotMail account, but my mailbox is still full. Why?

This is not just a HotMail issue. Deleting your e-mail messages doesn't make them disappear completely. It just sends them from your Inbox to a Deleted or Trash folder. The Deleted folder is a bit like the Windows Recycle Bin or a trash basket in your office. All the files are still in it; they're just marked for deletion. To clear your Deleted folder, click on the Empty instruction—in HotMail it's in the Deleted folder; in e-mail software such as Outlook Express, you right-click on the folder and select Empty Deleted.

I'm seeing a lot of weird clusters of punctuation. What's :-) all about?

It's another example of online shorthand, called a smiley or emoticon. Tilt your head to the left and look again—it looks like a smiley-face, doesn't it? Emoticons are useful tools for making people understand the mood you're in when you write a sentence. Here are a few useful emoticons—you'll see a lot more variants, but these will get you by.

: -)	a smile	; -)	a sly wink
: - X	my lips are sealed	: - (	a sad face
: - o	I'm shocked!	: - O	I'm very shocked!

What is netiquette?

Netiquette is a cute term for Internet etiquette—but there's nothing cute about showing good manners online. Netiquette is the only way not to offend people as you start to exchange e-mail with them. The three basic rules of netiquette are: don't spam, don't flame and don't shout. **Spamming** is sending lots of unwanted e-mail. **Flaming** is sending angry or offensive e-mail—an easy mistake to fall into if you write e-mail when you're tired or emotional. **Shouting** IS TYPING A SENTENCE OR ENTIRE MESSAGE IN UPPER-CASE LETTERS—a trick that makes an e-mail very hard to read. The best way to avoid all these faux pas? Take a deep breath and read over your e-mail before you send it.

 OW WHERE DO I GO?!

CONTACTS	PUBLICATIONS
The core rules of netiquette www.albion.com/netiquette/corerules.html	**Better, Faster E-Mail** By Joan Tunstall
Help.com's e-mail section help.cnet.com/cat/3/325 (no www. needed)	**Writing Effective E-Mail** By Nancy Flynn and Tom Flynn
	E-Mail for Dummies By John R. Levine

CHAPTER 3 ON THE WORLD WIDE WEB

IT'S A WILD WORLD WIDE WEB OUT THERE,
FULL OF NEW SIGHTS AND SOUNDS AND VIDEO
AND NEWS AND ENTERTAINMENT AND . . .
THE LIST GOES ON. SURF'S UP! SO WAX DOWN
YOUR MOTHERBOARD (WE DON'T MEAN THAT
LITERALLY!) AND GET READY TO HANG TEN ON
THE WEB.

ON THE WORLD WIDE WEB

Web pages— what are they?

The building blocks of the World Wide Web

Like the pages in a magazine or book, Web pages contain words and pictures, put together in some kind of design. Also, like magazine pages, some Web pages are a lot fancier than others. But that's where the comparisons end. In a magazine, you're pretty much limited to flipping pages and filling in crossword puzzles. Web pages are **interactive**, meaning that you can interact with the information. For example, you can use your computer mouse and click on links that take you to other Web sites or Web games.

Almost all Web pages are larger than what you first see. Your **browser** (the software that lets you navigate the Web) acts like a periscope on the page. What you're seeing is the top left of the Web

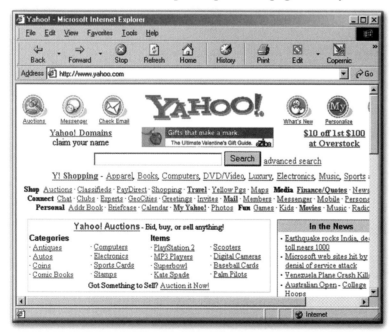

page—there could be a lot more down below or to the side. You can tell by looking for **scroll bars** (arrow keys) at the far right as well as at the bottom of your monitor's screen. Click one of the arrows and watch your view of the Web page shift along. In the scroll bar, you'll also see a gray moving rectangle that shows your place on the page you're viewing.

Congratulations! You've just navigated a Web page.

There's more to this page than meets the eye! Use your mouse to click on the scroll bar arrows to see what else is on the Web page.

 ## ASK THE EXPERTS

Why are those things at the edge of the screen called scroll bars?

The techies who invented them thought that sliding down a page worked a bit like reading a scroll (those ancient rolls of parchment the Egyptians and Romans used to read)—only a bit was visible at a time.

A Web page I visited played a tune through my computer speakers. How?

Well, it's simple and complicated. Behind every Web page you read is a list of coded instructions that tells your Web browser (software that helps your computer navigate the Web) what to show. These instructions can also tell your browser to load other files from the Web page too—including music and video clips—and then use a program on your hard disk to play them. Wild stuff!

FIRST PERSON DISASTER STORY

The print job that wouldn't die

I found a really interesting Web page when I was surfing the Net in my local library, so I figured I'd print it out. I hit the Print button. Nothing happened. I figured that there was a bug in the software. I hit it again. No problem. A few minutes later, the librarian came over to the computer with a stack of papers. "Here's your printout, two copies" she said. There were 30 color copies there—which the library charged me $1.00 a sheet for. I didn't realize the Web page I was looking at was 15 pages long!

Now I only print exactly what I want: I hold down the left mouse button and drag down to the bottom of the selection so what I want to print is highlighted. Then click on File menu and Print. In the Print dialog box, I click on the Print Selection button, and click OK. It's a bit geeky, but it saves a fortune in copying fees.

Mack T., Marcus Hook, Pennsylvania

Web page anatomy

What's all that
stuff on my
Web page?

Web sites like to cram as much as possible onto their Web page. That can lead to a lot of stuff on the page—which at first glance can be confusing. The key to getting comfortable on the Web is to move the mouse around and click on things. You can't go far wrong—if you make a "mistake," there's always a Back button to click. Here's a quick guide to some of the most common elements on a Web page.

A Links: The very core of the Web is linking to other Web sites. Click on a link (underlined text) and you could be whisked away to another Web page—or another page could pop up in addition to the one you're already at. Not all links are obvious. Sure, most text links are blue text that's underlined, but any text color or picture could be a link. Tip: Move your mouse around the page; if the mouse cursor changes shape to a pointing finger, it's over a link.

B List boxes: These little boxes have down arrows at their right, and they're used to help navigate complex Web sites. Click on the arrow to reveal a list of possible places to visit—then click your mouse on one to select it. You usually press a button labeled "Go" to go there.

C Text box: Click in these, and you can type stuff into a Web page. These are used for searching sites or submitting your e-mail address or name at a site. Click the button next to the box to send the information to the Web site.

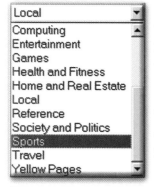

B

D Images: Pictures on Web sites are usually called graphics or images, and they're in one of two file formats—called GIF or JPEG (pronounced "jif" and "jaypeg"). They're often not just eye candy. This one is an image map—a picture that contains several links that take you to other Web pages.

E Menu: Thanks to a little smart programming, some text on some sites pops out into a menu. It's a neat trick—just move your mouse over the text, and pop! Down slips a whole list of links to click on.

F Tabs: One way that Web designers cram a lot into a small space is to put tabs at the top of an area of the screen. Like those labels at the top of manila file folders, they show what's contained within. Click on one, and boom! you're looking at something different in that space.

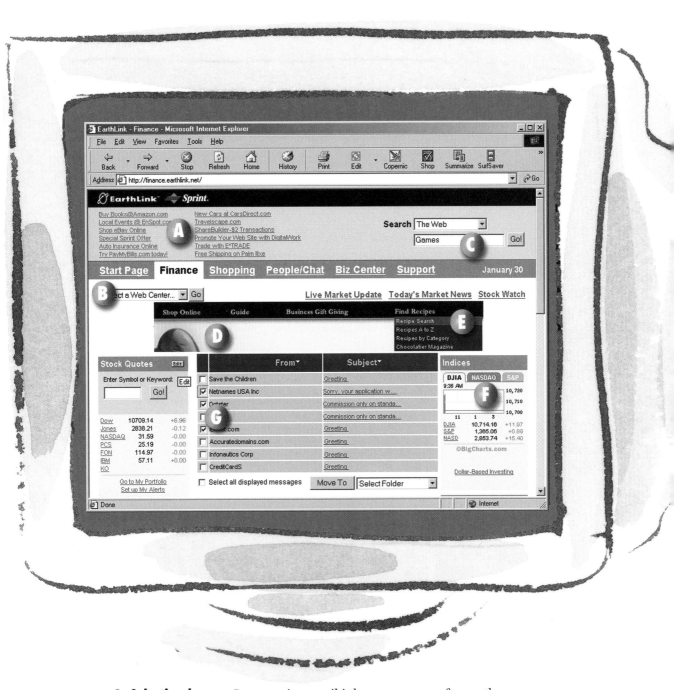

G Selection boxes: Common in e-mail inboxes or survey forms, these little square boxes let you select several items on a list. Once you've clicked in one, a check mark appears (click again to remove the check mark). Once you've checked off all you want to, look for a list box or button that tells you what to do next.

search engines

Find what you're looking for

Whether you're doing a crossword, acting as the phone-a-friend on *Who Wants to be a Millionaire?* or doing a term paper, you want answers fast. The answers are out on the Web somewhere, and a search engine is the way to find them.

Think of a **search engine** as a digital encyclopedia ready to sift through thousands of Web pages that its indexers have selected and organized to get your answer. The indexes are built by special software that follows link after link on Web pages and compiles the information into a huge database. The neat software that does the searches also works differently from search engine to search engine. The bottom line here? Find a search engine you like and stick to it.

How do you start a search? All you need to do is to type in one or two **key words** (the most descriptive words you can use, e.g., rubber rafts) about what you're after. Within seconds, the search engine gives you a long list of links on a **results page.** Each link on the results page will show a Web address, some with an excerpt of what's on the page, others with just the title of the page. If you see something on the results page that matches what you're looking for, just click on the link and you're whisked off to that page. For search tips see the next page.

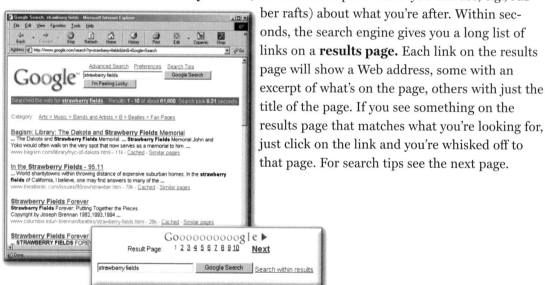

Get results! Here are the results of a search at the popular Web site Google.com. Scroll through the first page, and if you don't see what you're looking for, click on Next to see the following page of results.

STEP BY STEP: SEARCH SMART

Follow these steps to get the result you want.

1. Pick your engine   There are many choices of search engines. No one site is good for every search. Yahoo and AskJeeves are great for researching general topics. Google and AltaVista are better for very specific information.

2. Don't keep trying   If you don't find what you're looking for in the first list of items and links, enter a different set of key words or move on to another search site.

3. Choose your words   Most search engines do a poor job looking for a single key word. Increase the number of key words to increase the scope of your search. Pick the words well, and double-check your spelling.

4. Use key words that work   Type in Strawberry Fields as words in a search box, and you could get W.C. Fields and ~~~~rry in your results. See below for tips.

SEARCH TIPS

. few expert tricks that help weed out irrelevant ~m your searches.

uote marks around key phrases (as in "Strawberry ~~). In most search engines, this will exclude irrelevant results, such as pages that mention walking through fields eating strawberry jam.

2. Exclude some key words using a minus sign. If you're looking for Ringo's solo work, but find the first results are all Beatles sites, type in this: Ringo –Beatles and most search engines will throw out pages containing the word Beatles. (A few search sites prefer you to use the word NOT instead of the minus sign—as in Ringo NOT Beatles. But the minus is much more popular).

your entry to the Web

Pull up a virtual chair and make yourself at home on the Net

Getting onto the Internet is a bit like leaving home for the first time. It's a huge and exciting world out there, and it can be overwhelming. Relax, it's fun, really. Here's a way to make it manageable: always start your online adventures from the same page. Chances are your Internet Service Provider will provide you with a **home page** (the first page that is displayed when you launch your browser). These home pages are sometimes called **portals** because they're designed as entryways to parts of the Web that they hope will be useful to you—for instance, links to the weather sites and stock prices, as well as news sites for breaking stories. They also have message forums where you can exchange messages with other people in the Web equivalent of a message board. (For more on that see page 79.) Also expect search boxes and directories of links to other Web sites.

Portals like iVillage let you pick the information you see—a process that Web folks call personalizing.

The cool thing about portal sites is that you can often personalize them. If you want to read entertainment news, avoid politics, and see only the stocks in your portfolio, you can. But you'll have to sign up first, which involves entering your name and e-mail address at the site and giving yourself a password. If you're ready to move on from your service provider's portal page, check out general-interest portals such as My Yahoo or My Excite.

# ASK THE EXPERTS

How does My Yahoo remember my personalized settings?

Instead of keeping reams of files on everyone, My Yahoo and other Web servers put a tiny bit of data about you on your hard drive. This tiny bit of data is called a **cookie**. It allows Yahoo and others to recognize you and your personal interests when you return to your portal site, so it can serve up your personal settings.

Do portal sites keep track of my browsing habits to sell to advertisers?

The same cookie that helped personalize your portal can also be used to keep track of the pages you view on the portal site. Many sites use this information to figure out which pages are most popular on their site, but they don't tell advertisers who you are and where you've been.

How do I make a portal site my home page?

First visit the site, then tell your browser to make it your home page. If Internet Explorer is your browser, click the Tools menu and Internet Options. Under Home page, click the Use Current button. In Netscape Communicator, click on Edit, Preferences, and under Home page, click the Use Current Page button.

POPULAR PORTALS

MainPortals.com
http://mainportals.com
a listing of portals in many topics

My Yahoo
http://my.yahoo.com
general-interest portal

My Excite
http://my.excite.com
a general-interest portal

iVillage
http://www.ivillage.com
general women's-interest portal

downloading stuff

The Web is a place where instant gratification is almost possible. You can fill your hard drive with . . . well, anything that a hard drive can hold—music, software programs, games, screen savers, graphics and photographs, even movies.

The process of getting stuff from the Internet onto your hard disk is called **downloading**. Think of downloading as moving a house brick by brick from one place to another. Your computer gets bits of a computer file and has to reconstruct them on your hard disk. This takes time, especially if your Internet connection is a slow one, but the convenience is unbeatable. Some downloads (yes, it's a noun as well as a verb) are completely free. Some you must pay for before you download. But many of them are called **shareware**—files that are free to try but which you should pay for if you continue to use them after a trial period (usually 30 days). If you don't pay, some shareware downloads will stop working after their trial time is up, but most of them continue to work, with occasional reminders to register and pay.

One way that computer folk speed up the business of downloading is to **compress** files into what are called **archives** or **zip files**. Like taking the air out of a balloon, compressing files makes them smaller without really altering them. But you need a software program to restore them to full size once they're on your hard disk. Where to get it? From the Web of course. Type in **Winzip.com** or **Aladdinsys.com** (don't forget the "sys" after Aladdin), and click on the Download or Download Evaluation Version link. You'll be taken to a page with another link that offers to download the program when you click it. Make sure the link is labeled with your computer and operating system (Windows 98, Mac OS or whatever). Then, read on . . .

STEP BY STEP: HOW TO DOWNLOAD

The business of downloading starts by finding a link that leads to a file or program.

1. Before you download that first file, set up a folder in your browser to collect all your downloads. In fact, America Online already has one in place. (In My Computer, check under the C: hard drive for a folder called Downloads. If it's not there, check in the America Online folder). If you don't have one, make one: In My Computer, double-click on the C: hard drive and then right-click on a blank piece of screen. From the drop-down box, click on New, then Folder. When the folder appears, type in the name Downloads. Bingo! you have a special downloads file.

2. When you're in your browser ready to download a file, click on its link. A dialog box will appear, asking where to store the folder.

3. Click on Browse, and navigate to the Downloads folder you found or created in step 1.

4. Click on OK.

5. Once the download is complete, switch over to My Computer and double-click on the name of the new file.

6. From here on out, every time you click a download link, your browser will remember the last place you stored a download, so you won't have to go through all these steps again.

DOWNLOAD SITES

You can find all kinds of programs, games, screensavers, and other goodies to download at all kinds of Web sites. But here are some big Web sites devoted exclusively to providing you with downloads.

CNET's Download.com
www.download.cnet.com

Shareware.com
www.shareware.com

TUCOWs
www.tucows.com

now what do I do?

Answers to common questions

What's a Web directory?

Web directories are like the yellow pages—you browse for information in categories. You can compare and contrast different Web sites in these categories. The best way to describe a Web directory is by example—Yahoo. It's the biggest directory of them all. But just to confuse things, many popular search engine sites also have Web directories you can browse through—check out the directory links at Excite and Google to see for yourself.

When I visit some sites, they say I need a plug-in. What does that mean?

Your Web browser can do plenty of things without any help. It can display Web pages with text and pictures, it can play some kinds of sound files too. It can even run some pretty interesting programs written in a computer language called Java. But by itself, your browser can't play video files or some other programs written in other computer languages. To run these more exotic files and programs, your browser needs a helper program called a **plug-in.** Some of the most popular plug-ins are the video and audio program RealPlayer and the multimedia program players called Flash and Shockwave.

I'm looking for particular information on a Web page, but I can't find it. Help!

Don't get your eyes crossed scanning the small print. You can search for a word or phrase on any Web page and your browser will whisk you straight to it. Under the Edit menu, click on the Find (on this page) option—or hold down the Ctrl key on your keyboard and press the F key. You'll see a dialog box pop up. Enter the word you're looking for, and click the Find button. If that doesn't help, click the Find Next button.

I clicked on a link and landed at a Web page that says "404 Not Found" on it. What's up with that?

You just followed what's called a broken link—and it won't be the last time. The Web is full of broken links. They were either written wrong in the first place, or they originally pointed to a real Web page that was later removed. The Web is constantly changing, with new pages coming online and old pages being removed. It sure beats reruns on network television—but it can get frustrating sometimes.

I followed a link to a page with a scary message on it saying "Forbidden!" Is this a joke?

Nope. Some sites on the Web are strictly guarded. Like exclusive night clubs, they are for members only, and bouncers will make sure you don't get in. *The Wall Street Journal* (or www.WSJ.com), for example, won't show you its news stories unless you're a paid subscriber. Every time you access their Web page, you'll need to enter a user name and password before they show you the first screen. Not everything online is free!

Why do I get a "Page does not exist" message at a Web site when I know the page is there?

The first thing you need to do is double-check your typing. Web addresses aren't easy to type, and everyone makes mistakes sometimes—especially when there are numbers and letters mixed together. Make sure that the letter O is not really a zero, and that the letter "l" you typed isn't actually the number one. And remember that some Web sites are **case sensitive**, which means that they don't recognize a capital R as the same letter as a lowercase "r." Hey . . . nobody said the Web was smart. It's just full of fun and information.

 OW WHERE DO I GO?!

CONTACTS	PUBLICATIONS
Search Engine Watch www.searchenginewatch.com	**How the Internet Works Millennium Edition** By Preston Gralla
About.com www.about.com	**Sams Teach Yourself the Internet in 10 Minutes** By Galen Grimes
Download.com www.download.cnet.com	**Web Searching for Dummies** By Brad Hill

CHAPTER 4   RESEARCHING ONLINE

THE INFORMATION YOU WANT IS OUT THERE. WITH MORE THAN TWO BILLION WEB PAGES IN EXISTENCE, WITH NEW PAGES AND UPDATES HAPPENING EVERY DAY, THE INFORMATION IS POURING IN. THE TRICK, OF COURSE, IS FINDING IT, AND FIGURING OUT WHAT'S SOLID INFORMATION AND WHAT'S BOGUS. READ ON TO SORT IT ALL OUT.

RESEARCHING ONLINE

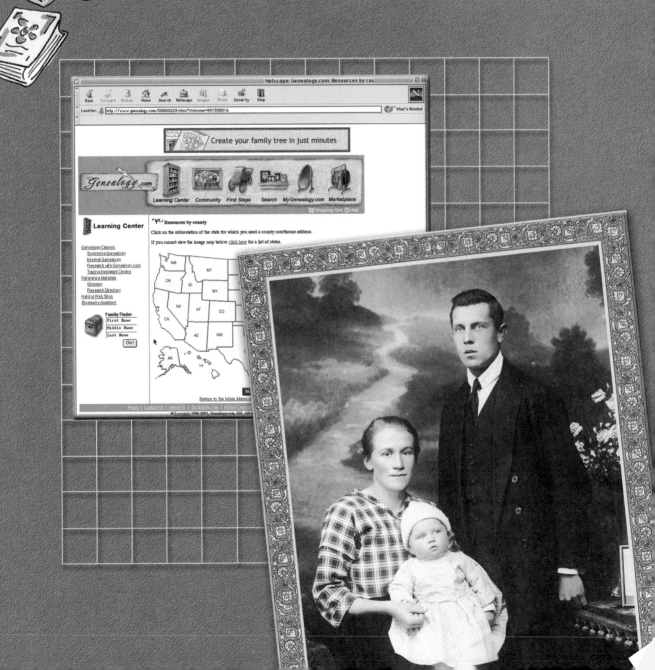

the Web library

The biggest library there is

Your best strategy for finding the information you want online is to find the right tools for the job. First try using a a search engine (see pages 64–65); next try a Web directory (see page 70). Search engines like Google and AltaVista are like librarians—they find the information for you. Directories like Yahoo and Lycos are like browsing the bookshelves yourself, looking through subject areas till you find the topic you're interested in.

There's another type of resource for Web information. They are called **specialized search sites** and they cover specific topics like news, medical information, academic research, and special interests. A good place to start all your specialized searches is Search.com (**www.search.com**). This provides a list of Yahoo-style directories, but each topic has one search box that searches a whole collection of specialized search sites. This one-box search of several sites is called **metasearching**. Geeky, yes, but who cares. It's so amazing when you try it.

FIRST PERSON   DISASTER STORY

Fact or urban legend?

I'm well known at work for being a news junkie with lots of interesting stories to share. So when I read an article about a proposed tax on Internet access, I jumped on the information. The article mentioned a bill before the Senate that would allow a surcharge on the phone bill for any line used for Internet connections. The article linked to a Government site where you could protest the bill, and included some other convincing details. The next day during my coffee break, I told a few people in my office about it, and they were amazed too. Later that afternoon, my boss sent me an e-mail message with a Web address in it. The link led to Hoaxbusters (http://hoaxbusters.ciac.org), which exposed the whole story as a fraud. It took me a while to win back my reputation after that!

Arthur B., St. Petersburg, Florida

STEP BY STEP: EVALUATING WEB SITES

Not all the information on the Web is accurate. The sites you find may contain outdated facts, misinformation, poor research, urban legends, propaganda and outright lies. How can you tell the good stuff? Use this checklist.

✔ **Check the grammar and spelling** Anything that reads as though it was dashed off in a hurry may have sloppy research too. Is the page you're reading grammatically incorrect? Are there spelling errors? If so, be on your guard.

✔ **Check out the author** Most articles online have bylines mentioning the writer's name. If you haven't heard of the writer or know his reputation, type the name into a search engine and see what else carries his byline.

✔ **Rate the publisher** Look at the Web address of any article you're evaluating. Is it a name you recognize, like *The New York Times* or CNN? If so, you can rest assured that some attempt has been made to check the facts, although even professional publishers and broadcasters make mistakes.

✔ **Evaluate the "spin"** No writing is ever completely impartial, so if an article online (or in print) is biased, try to figure out why. Some Web sites, for example, make money by referring their visitors to other Web sites. Comments about such-and-such site being "the best on the Web" should be taken with a grain of salt.

✔ **Check the sources** A good journalist or researcher always backs up his statements with sources. Check any article for sources and links to other reputable sites.

✔ **Check the date** In a book or newspaper, you can always see the publication date—so you know whether the information is current. On the Web, not every page carries the publication date. If you don't see a date, don't trust any figures the page calls "current."

current events

It's pouring rain outside, and the delivery boy has slung your daily newspaper into a puddle the size of Lake Superior. Where do you turn to get your news updates? To the Web, of course! Newspaper magnates and wire services were among the first commercial organizations to jump on the Web, so nowadays you can read all the headlines and news stories you want without getting black ink all over your fingers.

But where do you look? Well, most ISPs provide a few headlines on their home page that link to news services like Reuters and the Associated Press, the news wire services that sell stories to newspapers that don't have the reporting staff to cover them.

One of the best starting points is Yahoo's Daily News (**http://dailynews.yahoo.com**), which links you to the top stories at *The New York Times*, the Associated Press, ABC News, and many others. This service also provides links to local news sites and international news. If you're searching for a particular story, use Northern Light's Search News (**http://www.northernlight.com/news.html**), which lets you look for stories released in the past two hours, one day, or two weeks.

Of course, it's always worth checking out the Web site of your favorite news source from another medium—such as CNN's **CNN.com** and **CNNfn.com**, National Public Radio's **npr.org**, or the British Broadcasting Company's **bbc.co.uk**. If your favorite newspaper, TV channel, or radio station doesn't trumpet its Web address, search for it by name (or by region) at a Web directory such as **Google.com** or **Yahoo.com**.

I want to read just national news, entertainment, and local news. Must I wade through lots of pages to get it?

Not necessarily. Many news sites are pretty good about letting you personalize their pages to suit your tastes. You can tailor a personal page at **my.yahoo.com**, for example, to include news about sports, finance, and foreign news. How? Just click on the Edit button next to the news headlines, and when the list of news sources appears in the next page, click those checkboxes that interest you. Or you could visit a great site called **Crayon.net** (which is short for Create Your Own Newspaper Network), where you can compile your own news page from dozens of different sources—including the day's funny paper cartoons. To see your choice of news sources, visit **www.crayon.net/using/links.html**.

All the news that's fit to view. Crayon.net compiles news from a whole mass of different publications, turns the headlines into links, and slaps them onto a single page for your viewing pleasure.

The New York Times' site only lets in members. What's up with that?

Like many other sites, some newspapers want to save the good stuff for people who are prepared to register with them. They get a little demographic information to show their advertisers, you get free access to the information, and everyone's happy. At **NYTimes.com**, all you have to do is enter a little information about yourself and make up a password—all pretty straightforward stuff. A very few sites, including *The Wall Street Journal*, actually charge for membership to their site. If you're a subscriber to the hard copy (paper) edition, you pay a little bit extra to visit the site. If you're not a subscriber, the charge for visiting the online site is pretty steep.

old news

One of the best things about the Web is that it can store thousands and thousands of old articles. Many magazine publishers and newspapers are only too happy to extend the shelf life of their articles by putting them online. So you can find back issues of old publications, newsletters, and other articles online. In most cases, looking for an older article at a magazine or newspaper Web site is just like looking for a new story—you enter keywords in a search box and click on a link in the results page. Many newspaper and magazine Web sites charge you to view stories that are older than a year. (It's their way of defraying the cost of Web-server space.) The fees range from $1.00 to $2.50 per article.

If you don't know or care which publication wrote the article, enter a search at a Web site that specializes in news—Yahoo and Northern Light (**www.northernlight.com**) are particularly good at this. Northern Light compiles in-depth coverage of news stories into single pages that include analysis and links to relevant documents.

If you find that a lot of your research into old news stories isn't readily available online,

If you can't find an article anywhere else, try Electric Library. The service charges a subscription fee, but you get a 30-day free trial.

try a service that specializes in articles you can't get at any other Web site—the Electric Library (**www.elibrary.com**). This contains the full text of stories from more than 150 newspapers, hundreds of magazines and even transcripts of TV and radio shows, many of which aren't anywhere else online. The downside? After a 30-day free trial, Electric Library charges a monthly subscription fee. If you do a lot of research, however, the fee is worth it.

SK THE EXPERTS

Where can I find my favorite magazine online?

If the Web address isn't printed on the cover or if you can't find a copy, go straight to a site that lists online magazines—the "reading room" of the Internet Public Library (**www.ipl.org**). Click on the Magazines or Newspapers link at the IPL's home page, and select the region or the subject area the periodical covers. There are thousands of publications listed here. It's a safe bet you'll find what you're looking for.

I want to read old columns by my favorite columnist, William Safire. Can I do this online?

Sure thing—and the same goes for Dave Barry, Scott Adams, Dear Abby, Peggy Post and around 600 other scribes. Get over to Blue Eagle Commentary (**www.blueeagle.com**) for links to them all. Or enter their names in quotation marks (see page 88 for more search tips) at any search engine and see what turns up.

While researching WWII, I came across a strange Web page where I could post messages. What is that?

You stumbled onto a **message board**—a page within a Web site where you can post messages to the message board or respond to individual messages left on the board. But beware: Message boards are public forums, accessible by Internet users all over the world, so it's not a good idea to post a message and give your real name and e-mail address. Better to use a pen name, and if you want to give an e-mail address, get a second anonymous one. (See page 17).

academic research

Research your papers without paper

The Internet and the Web both took off because university academics wanted to share information. It's only natural that it should continue as a place to turn for serious research. So if you have a term paper due, your kids need homework help, or you just love to learn, fire up your Web browser, and read on.

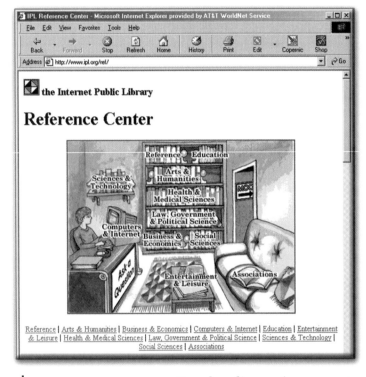

It looks like a library, and it works like one too. The Internet Public Library is a great resource for heavy-duty research or just casual browsing of the Web's great learning centers.

If your local library has a Web site, that's a great place to start your research. If not, turn to one of the virtual libraries on the Web. The Internet Public Library (**www.ipl.org**)and RefDesk (**www.refdesk.com**) are two great examples—each provides billions of links to useful research sites ranging from online encyclopedias to the Web sites of professional organizations.

If an encyclopedia entry is all you're looking for, then turn to the Encyclopaedia Britannica (**www.britannica.com**), Microsoft's Encarta (**www.encarta.com**), or all-Web resources like InfoPlease (**www.infoplease.com**) and Encyclopedia.com (**www.encyclopedia.com**) for your research. Search.com (**www.search.com**) provides a single place to search them all at one time.

There are hundreds of dictionaries and thesauruses online too—ranging from big names like Merriam-Webster to lesser-known technical lexicons like the Jargon File. To get the maximum number of results from your search, turn to OneLook (**www.onelook.com**), which searches for words in dozens of general and technical dictionaries. The results page provides links to the right page at all the dictionaries—you pick the dictionary you like best for the definition.

SK THE EXPERTS

I've found a Web site with some great facts on it, but there's no author name and I don't know the publisher. Can I use this information?

If it's not a recognized publisher or writer, it may be bogus information. Anyone grading a paper will reject a source like this. Don't risk your grades on this.

How do I cite a Web site in the bibliography of my paper?

Web entries must include the Web address and the date you viewed the page (since Web addresses and the contents of Web pages may change). The Modern Language Association of America (MLA) style guide recommends you format entries like this: Author. Title. Date of publication. Date you read the page and the Web address. An example would look like this:

Slatella, Michelle. A Quest of Modest Aims. Feb 8, 2001. April 1, 2001.
<http://www.nytimes.com/2001/02/08/technology/08SHOP.html>

I heard you can get a whole book online for free. Is that true?

Yes, you can. Usually they are older books that aren't restricted by copyright anymore, including Shakespeare, Mark Twain, and Lewis Carroll. Lots of universities are banding together to put books online in an international effort called the Gutenberg Project, named for the inventor of movable type. The collection is spread across lots of different Web sites, but you can enter an author name, book name, or subject at the Internet Public Library or at the University of Virginia's Electronic Text Center (**http://etext.lib.virginia.edu**) to find them. (Newer books online are called e-books, and you usually have to pay a fee before you can download them.)

medical information

Know what your doctor knows

There's no substitute for a good relationship with a good doctor—but that's not always possible given time restraints, and it's not a good idea to bug a doctor with every medical question you have. So if you want to find out good medical information and broaden your knowledge about treatment options, fortunately you can turn to the Internet.

There are some great resources on the Web, but you don't want to trust your health to unreliable sources, so here are a few pointers to finding the best sites. Some respected medical clinics provide great Web resources—including the Mayo Clinic's **mayoclinic.com** and Johns Hopkins' **Intelihealth.com**. And for a little more breadth and depth, visit **HealthWeb.org**. This cross between a directory and a *Consumer Reports* of online health resources has bazillions of links to sites that have been checked out and evaluated as useful.

If you know the name of your illness and can spell it (hey, fibromyalgia and toxoplasmosis aren't easy words to type!), you can find out about it from any search engine's results. If you're not so sure, check out a Web directory like Google's or Yahoo's. Sort through the affected body system (eye disorders, sleep disorders, and so on) and see what you turn up.

This hit-or-miss approach can turn up some less-than-useful sites, but it's a great way to find alternative medicine sites and support groups that professional medical sites may not include. For the official word from the medical profession, sites like the Mayo Clinic's, HealthWeb, and the other sites on our list are the places to go.

ASK THE EXPERTS

How can I check out the effects of prescription drugs?

Good for you! More people should be aware of the doses, side effects, and interactions between medications. Intelihealth and the Mayo Clinic's Web site have great search tools that provide you with background information from drug companies and other informed sources—and links to question-and-answer sessions.

I'm about to travel abroad. How do I find out what diseases to avoid in foreign lands?

The Centers for Disease Control has a special travelers' health section that will prove invaluable. It tracks all kinds of public health issues, outbreaks of diseases, and inoculation recommendations for numerous countries. Go to **http://www.cdc.gov/travel/** for this information. And bon voyage.

MEDICAL RESOURCES

HealthWeb
http://www.healthweb.org/
Lots of information resources, selected by impartial medical professionals for the quality of their information.

InteliHealth
http://www.intelihealth.com
Johns Hopkins University's excellent and easy to understand collection of journal databases, a medical dictionary, and expert Q&As.

Martindale's Health Science Guide
http://www-sci.lib.uci.edu/HSG/
HSGuide.html
Extensive database of health-related information, news and references.

Mayo Clinic
www.mayoclinic.com
The respected clinic's Web site does a great job of making health and medicine issues easy to understand.

Thrive Online
http://www.thriveonline.oxygen.com
Expert advice and communities devoted to health, medicine, and fitness.

WebMD
http://www.webmd.com
News, chat forums, and consumer updates on health resources, aimed at the public and professionals alike.

genealogy research

Your family tree is somewhere in the Web

You can go online to be part of the cutting edge of technology—but you can use it to delve into your past too. For the past few decades, genealogists have been putting historical, hard-to-find data online, such as 19th-century ship manifests from Europe to America. Some genealogy sites charge a fee for the really useful information—you sign up with your credit card and they charge you for the premium information you ask for. But plenty of sites offer free information and free services to get you started. So instead of plowing through obscure volumes of civic records, you can go online and build your family tree. Here are a few starting points.

Ancestry.com gives you a quick leg up into the world of researching your genealogy online, with useful databases and message boards where you can share your findings or ask for help from distant relatives.

www.ancestry.com

With some great tips and a nice selection of free databases, Ancestry.com is a good place to start. Even before signing up for a free membership, you can search for ancestors by name and check out census, military, and vital records (births, deaths, and marriages).

www.familysearch.com

Here's an Internet service from a group that specializes in genealogy—the Church of the Latter-day Saints, also known as the Mormons. Once you sign up for a free membership, you can browse records of census, property records, voting registration, and veterans groups—and a whole lot more. You can also build up a starter family tree, once you've registered. The Mormon church asks you to create and submit a family tree in the standard GEDCOM format (a special computer type of family history), but this is optional. If you do, your records will be stored in the church's archives in the Granite Mountain Records Vault in Utah.

www.cyndislist.com

Ready to cast your net wider? Cyndi's got what you need—a vast collection of genealogy links (tens of thousands of them). It's a bit overwhelming for beginners, but you can't fault this site's research into Web resources.

www.genealogy.com

There's a good selection of beginner's orientation information at Genealogy.com, and a friendly list of online resources you can tap. Genealogy.com would love you to buy their software (it's heavily advertised at the site), but you get plenty of free help here.

The neat menu system on Genealogy.com's home page pops up myriad helpful articles and databases for you to use to scale your family tree.

finding people

Reach out and find anyone with your mouse

Your old college roommate. Your first love. That degenerate bum of a cousin who skipped town owing you money. They all have something in common—you'd love to get back in touch with them.

That's where the Web comes in. There are dozens of sites devoted to the old-fashioned type of networking—getting people together. All you need to get started is a name (though a town or full address can be handy). Go to any of the sites listed at the bottom of this page. (Start with Search.com, then click on a link called People, which searches a whole bunch of these sites at once).

Decide what contact medium you want to use. If you're comfortable cold-calling, choose the phone lookup option. If you'd prefer a low-impact method for your first inquiry, pick an e-mail lookup. Enter whatever information you have, and sit back. In a while, you'll get a list of all the John and Jane Does in the States and beyond. From here on out, it's up to you. These sites will find the e-mail or phone numbers and postal addresses of people you name.

The first step to reestablishing contact is to enter a name at **Search.com,** then click on a line called People, which searches dozens of different sites for e-mail addresses, phone numbers, and other contact info.

AnyWho
www.anywho.com

InfoSpace
www.infospace.com

InfoUSA
www.infousa.com

Switchboard
www.switchboard.com

WhoWhere
www.whowhere.lycos.com

Yahoo People
People.yahoo.com

ASK THE EXPERTS

I found a phone number in my pocket, but I don't know whose it is. Can the Web help me find it?

Sure. There are several places where you can do a reverse lookup—that is, enter a number and find whom it belongs to. Try **InfoSpace**, **InfoUSA**, or **AnyWho**—or visit **Search.com**'s Reverse Lookup section and search all three at once. You should get a street address, and maybe even maps and driving directions.

My buddy's name is John Smith. How can I be sure the listing I got is his?

Well, you can't. If you've got a good long-distance plan, block off a weekend and call them all. If not, look up the e-mail addresses and try a polite inquiry to all the results. Keep it short and sweet. "If you're the John Smith who used to drag race with me at Altamont, drop me a line. If not, sorry to disturb, but please let me know so I can cross you off my list."

I still can't find the person I'm looking for. What are my other options?

Here's a good one. Use a regular search engine that covers a lot of the Web (**Google.com** or FAST's **alltheweb.com**) and enter the name of your buddy in quotation marks. If they've made the jump online with a personal Web page, or appeared in the news, or been made employee of the week at a Web company, you may find their name on a Web page somewhere. Most Web pages provide some contact information—and that's your next step in getting back in touch.

Where are your high school and college friends now? Use the Internet and find out.

now what do I do?

Answers to common questions

How can I reduce the number of irrelevant results from my searches? Any seach tips?

There are three tricks to searching smart. First, pick the right words to search for—put in two or three words and you're more likely to get good results. Second, enclose "names" or "phrases" in quotation marks—this forces the search engine to treat them as phrases. And finally, exclude words that introduce irrelevant results—at most sites, you do this by inserting a minus sign. If your search for Sgt. Pepper, for example, brings up a dozen karaoke sites, search for "Sgt. Pepper"–karaoke, and you'll lose the links to karaoke sites.

What is Usenet?

Usenet is a loose kind of Internet community that's been around since way before the Web was born. You can find archives of their message forums (called newsgroups) at a site like **groups.google.com**. At this site, you can type in your key words and find informal discussions that aren't published or sanctioned by any corporation. It's a way to get the point of view of consumers when you're thinking about trying a new product or service.

Is there one search engine that covers all the Web?

No, there isn't. Even the search engine with the biggest reach— **Alltheweb.com**—covers only about a third of the estimated two billion pages on the Web. But you can increase your reach by using a metasearch site. **Search.com** is the easiest name to remember, but several other sites do the same thing—including Dogpile (**www.dogpile.com**) and Mamma (**www.mamma.com**).

I want to save my results. Is there an easy way to do this?

Yes there is—but you must download a program from **www.copernic.com** first. Copernic 2001 is available free, and it's a pretty amazing tool. It metasearches a dozen of the best search sites and presents the results to you in a huge list. You can delete the results you don't like, because this list is not at a Web page, it's on your computer. You can save the good ones to read later. And it even solves the problem of results that lead to pages that don't exist. You can click on Copernic 2001's Validate button and the program will go out and check that the page still exists. If not, it will remove the dud result from your list. This is a great tool for serious researchers who want to keep a record of where they found their information

I read a convincing posting on a medical message board that recommended something my doctor never mentioned. What should I do?

You have to be careful about all information you read online. Your doctor studied for years to get a degree. Do you know the qualifications of the guy who posted the message on the Web? Do a little background check on the writer (see page 75), and double-check the information that he wrote. Think like Dustin Hoffman and Robert Redford in *All the President's Men*—if you can get three independent sources to say the same thing, there may be something in it. But don't gamble your health on anything. Once you've done your research, take up the issue with your doctor.

 **N**OW WHERE DO I GO?!

CONTACTS	PUBLICATIONS
How search engines work http://www.learnthenet.com/english/ animate/search.html	**Researching Online for Dummies** By Reva Basch and Mary Ellen Bates
Research it! http://www.itools.com/research-it/ research-it.html	**Find It Online: The Complete Guide to Online Research** By Alan M. Schlein
	Doing Internet Research: Critical Issues and Methods for Examining the Net Edited by Steve Jones

CHAPTER 5   SHOPPING ONLINE

YES, VIRGINIA, YOU CAN ACTUALLY BUY THINGS
ON THE INTERNET. HOW? JUST GO ONLINE ,
FIND WHAT YOU WANT, TYPE IN YOUR CREDIT
CARD NUMBER AND MAILING ADDRESS AND
PRESTO, IT'S AT YOUR DOORSTEP. READ ON TO
LEARN JUST HOW EASY AND SAFE ONLINE
SHOPPING CAN BE.

SHOPPING ONLINE

at the Web store

Remember the last time you went shopping, found a convenient parking place right away, got immediate assistance in the store, bought your items, and had them delivered to your car? No? Well, that's how Web shopping works (sort of)—and the best of it is, you can shop anytime you want without elbowing your way through a crowd.

All you need to shop online is a Web browser (see page 24), Internet access (see page 20) and a credit card (see pages 94-95). When you're equipped with these, you can order almost anything online, from books and CDs to flowers and even cars.

Where do you find these goods online? At an **e-commerce** site—a Web site devoted to electronic commerce (a techie way of saying, "selling you stuff online"). There are sites operated by familiar real-world retailers, such as Toys R Us—look for **toysrus.com**. And there are also Web-only "stores," such as **amazon.com**, which exist only on the Web. A number of major manufacturers have their own sites so you can buy goods directly from them online—for example, **dell.com** for Dell computers. There are catalog vendors, such as **victoriassecret.com** and **landsend.com**. There are auction sites (more on those on pages 100-101). And finally, there are online malls, where you can go to one site and shop for all different kinds of stuff from different vendors. Try **shopping.yahoo.com**.

# ASK THE EXPERTS

How do you actually buy something online?

When you find something you want to buy at a shopping site, you click on a button labeled Buy or Purchase and the site takes you to a page it calls a **shopping cart**. Like a real-life cart, this page "holds" the products you want to buy. If you want to purchase more products, you can click on another button and carry on looking around the online store. When you're ready to complete your purchase, click on the Proceed to Checkout button, and you'll go to another page, where you enter your mailing and billing information (see page 94 for safe billing).

What if I don't like something I've bought online?

Like regular stores, online stores have returns policies. Very few sites have an "all sales are final" policy, so you can shop with confidence. But before you buy anything, click around the site till you find the returns policy. Read it carefully. Does the company charge a **restocking fee** (a handling charge for taking back returned goods, usually 10 percent of the original purchase price)? Does the company cover return shipping charges for damaged goods?

Do sites keep track of my shopping habits?

Yes—but then again, so do local bricks-and-mortar stores like Radio Shack and Toys R Us. When they ask for your phone number and/or address, they want the information so that they can send you direct-marketing mailers about sales or new merchanidise you might like. When you buy things online, sites use little text files called **cookies** on your computer to identify you, and also keep track of your purchases so they can recommend similar products to you later. Some people don't like this, others appreciate the recommendations—it's a matter of taste.

IS THAT A GOOD DEAL?

You often find very attractive prices online—10 percent or more off the regular price. This doesn't always mean a good deal, though. You have to pay shipping and handling charges on almost every purchase you make—and they can really add up. Sometimes it's worth paying a little extra for the convenience of shopping from your desk, but don't assume that you'll always be getting a great deal just because you see a good price.

safety with credit cards

Shopping with peace of mind

The standard currency on the Internet is the credit card. That's because you can enter your credit card number yourself and the vendor can get paid electronically. The good news is that nearly all Web vendors have secure purchase pages, meaning that when you enter your credit card number it is **encrypted** (tech speak for scrambled in code) so no one else but the vendor can read it. Here are some tips to make your purchases even safer.

Shop only on secure Web pages. All Web vendor sites are open for surfing. However, when you are ready to enter your personal data on the purchase page, check for these two visual clues to make sure the sight is secure.

1. If the Web address at the top of the purchase page begins with https:// instead of http://, that purchase page is secure. If there's no "s" there, it's not secure.

2. Look for a little symbol of a padlock at the bottom of your browser's window. If it's open, you're not on a secure purchase page. If it's closed, you're safe.

Never send credit card information via e-mail. Remember, e-mail messages are like postcards. They are simply not confidential enough for important financial information.

USE YOUR CREDIT CARD SAFELY

An alternative to credit cards is a transaction site, such as PayPal (**www.paypal.com**) or eMoneyMail (**emoneymail.com**). These sites act as middlemen for your online purchases so that people without credit cards—and those who don't want to spread their credit card numbers all over the Web—can spend their cash online.

FEWER WORRIES

Online security experts agree: designate one credit card for all your Web purchases. Ask the issuing credit card company about your liability. Federal law limits your liability to $50 if there is fraudulent use of your credit card. Some waive that liability—especially if you report any suspicious charges promptly. Keep your designated card's credit limit low. Even though your liability is limited, it's a nuisance to have some credit card fraud running up lots of charges. You can review the policies and fees for credit cards at **creditcardsearchengine.com**. Don't even put this credit card in your wallet—keep it in a safe place and use it only for online purchases.

Once you've got your online card, keep a log of which Web stores know your credit card number. Most online sites store your credit card number for future purchases. If you see suspicious activity on the card, you'll be able to report the companies to the credit card issuer. And if you have to cancel a credit card because of an electronic theft of its number, you'll know which stores to visit to update your card number.

ORDERING OVER THE PHONE

Contrary to popular opinion, shopping over the phone can be riskier than shopping on the Web. Nobody can eavesdrop on a secure Web connection; you can't say that about a cell-phone or portable-phone call. To be safe, use a regular, land-line telephone for credit card purchases. Don't get too anxious. Remember, credit card companies and federal law limit your liability.

finding the right store

Directions to the Web's stores and malls

Sitting in front of a computer isn't quite the same as shopping in a real store. Sure, you can't browse the aisles and touch the merchandize, but the Web can do things that no salesclerk will do, such as comparison shop to get you the best prices, find rare products that don't get shelf space in regular stores, and point to impartial reviews to make sure you're buying exactly the right product.

Your first stop should be a **personal shopper site** that compares prices from different online stores. MySimon (**www.mysimon.com**) is one of the best, as is **www.pricewatch.com** and **www.pricegrabber.com**. At these sites, you click on the type of goods you're looking for—clothes, cars, toys, or whatever—and you'll get links to products. You can also type a model number or manufacturer's name or key words into a search box to find just what you want.

Once you've found a product you're interested in buying, MySimon provides a list of places to buy it, sorted with the best prices first.

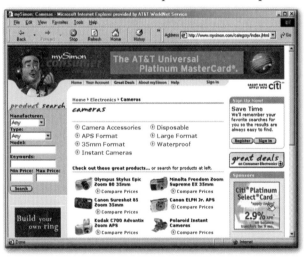

Click on the link with the best price, and zoom! You're at a shopping site where you can place the order. Personal shopper sites are great tools for researching the shopping sites with the best prices. If you're buying computers or other electronic goods, you might want to try **Computers.com**. It works like MySimon's price comparison service but focuses on electronics.

SK THE EXPERTS

Where can I find unbiased consumer advice on the Web?

At the bottom of each MySimon (**www.mysimon.com**) category, for example, are links to buyers' guides written by unbiased consumer writers (not salespeople on commission).

I prefer to deal with companies I know. Why should I shop online?

You can deal with companies you know and still shop on the Web. Most large companies with brick-and-mortar stores also sell things online—Walmart, Barnes & Noble, and the kids' store Zany Brainy all have online stores. (Try **www.walmart.com**, **www.bn.com**, and **www.zanybrainy.com**.) And the same goes for big-ticket manufacturers too—you can buy a Dell computer or a Saturn sedan direct from the manufacturer's Web site (at **www.dell.com** or **www.saturn.com**).

I want to shop online from my favorite catalog. Is there a Web directory that will have its Web address?

Naturally! The directories at Yahoo, Google, and Excite list this type of store in their shopping directories. Just click on their shopping links until you see a listing for catalogs.

ONLINE STORES

Some big Web stores exist only on the Web. Here are some of the best known.

Amazon.com
www.amazon.com
Books, movies, music, auctions, and a mix of other goods.

Buy.com
www.buy.com
An online superstore with good discounts and a wide range of products.

Half.com
www.half.com
An online second-hand store with some great prices on nearly new goods—and links to other stores if you want to buy new.

Shop@AOL
Shopping.aol.com
Think of this as a mall on the Web—it has many stores all collected under one Web address.

Yahoo Shopping
Shopping.yahoo.com
A virtual mall of stores with names you know (Target, Eddie Bauer, etc.) and names you don't.

purchasing

I'll take it!— but how?

Okay, you've found a Web store and you've gone through the links to the various products, and there's one you want to buy. Now what? For first-timers, it's a bit daunting, but you'll get the hang of it. All Web sites have pretty easy directions to walk you through the actual purchase of online items. Here's a breakdown of the process.

1. Click on the link, next to the product you want, that contains the words Purchase or Add to Cart. Most online stores keep track of the products you want in a Web page they call a **shopping cart**.

2. The shopping cart page lists the item and its availability. If you want to buy more than one, you can adjust the quantity here. If you change your mind, you can delete an item from your cart. Most sites don't tell you the full price you'll pay up front—they need to know the shipping address so they can calculate postal costs and local taxes. But there's almost always a link to follow so you get some idea of the total.

3. At this point you can click on a link to keep on shopping. Don't worry, the site will keep track of your purchases while you continue **browsing** (going back to search through more products).

4. When you've done with looking around and are ready to buy, click on the Proceed to Checkout button. You'll now be prompted to **sign in** (type in your name and e-mail address and a password for that site) to the site. All online shops need you to register. That way, they can store your shipping

address and other details so you don't have to keep typing them in.

5. If you're buying at a site for the first time, you'll need to put in all your shipping information and enter credit card information (see page 94). (Most Web companies know some people are nervous about this and will give an option of phoning in your credit card number.)

6. Once you've entered your shipping address and chosen your mailing rate (express or regular delivery), the site calculates the full amount, including shipping and taxes, and asks you to confirm the purchase. Only when you've seen the full shipping costs and clicked the confirmation will your order go through.

PURCHASE PROBLEMS

Some things can go wrong with every purchase. Here are some common problems and solutions.

You change your mind after you make the purchase.
Most companies let you change your mind before fulfilling the order. Some provide a phone number and some ask for e-mail cancellations.
To do: Always print out the confirmation page that the company e-mails to you and check out a Web site's cancellation policy.

You change your mind after you receive the goods.
Very few online sales are final. You should be able to return goods for a refund. However, you'll usually be responsible for return shipping costs.
To do: Always check the returns policy of a site before you buy from it. Pay close attention to phrases like **restocking fee**—where a company keeps a portion of the purchase price to process returns, so you don't get a full refund.

The goods arrive damaged.
You can always get a refund or replacement—but check beforehand to see if there are any strings attached to the returns.

online auctions

**Going…
going… gone!**

Imagine that you've got an attic full of stuff you don't need. (It's easy if you try!) Now imagine that you're ready to get rid of all that stuff. Too overwhelming an undertaking? Turn to the Web and put your treasures up for auction online. Once you've sold off your stuff, you can bid on other people's treasures and fill your attic up again!

Sure, dealing with strangers can be a leap of faith—especially when it takes two or three weeks to complete a sale (counting the auction, sending payment, waiting for checks to clear, and mailing out and/or receiving the goods). But auction sites like **eBay.com** and **auctions.yahoo.com** have good self-policing systems in place to keep things moving. Ebay has been up since 1997. It now has some 23 million registered users who buy and sell anything from baseball cards to antique table linens to used cars.

Here's how it works. After viewing the goods for sale, buyers type in a bid and it appears on the site. Other bidders will do the same. At the end of the auction, the auction site sends an e-mail to the highest bidder and to the seller. They then figure out how to handle payment and shipping.

FIRST PERSON ␣ DISASTER STORY

Patience is a virtue online, too

It was the first time I sold anything at an online auction, and I watched the bidding for the last half hour. The bids got higher and higher. What a thrill! And when it was over, I got the e-mail address of the high bidder from the site and sent a message saying "Congratulations!" and asking what to do next. No reply. Next day, still no reply. I sent another message, then another—each one getting more and more ticked off. Three days went by and I posted negative feedback about this buyer. The following day, I got a message from the bidder saying that his kid had gotten sick right after the auction closed, and he had been away from his computer for a week nursing the poor guy. I felt like a real heel and kicked myself for being so impatient. These things can take time, I learned.

Pat W., White Haven, Pennsylvania

STEP BY STEP: AUCTIONING

1. Sign up with an online auction site. Click on the site's Join link and enter your real name, address, and e-mail address. If you're selling, you'll need to enter a credit card number or arrange to send a check to cover **insertion fees** (charges made for listing items for auction—usually less than a dollar) and **commissions** (generally 2 to 5 percent of the sale price paid to the auction site).

2. Once you've registered, you can put up items for sale. Sellers should set a realistic **starting price** (aim low to encourage bidders, but not so low you'd be upset to sell on the opening bid). You can also set a **reserve price** so you don't have to sell at too low a price. Bidders will be told if they haven't hit the reserve price. Most sites let you insert photographs, so check for instructions. It's helpful to find out how much it will cost to ship the item, and you should list that in your description.

3. Buyers can search for items by entering key words (such as Mickey Mantle baseball card or Chippendale chair) in the site's Search box. The resulting list is sorted by date, with the auctions about to end at the top. Auctions usually last 5 to 7 days. If an item seems interesting, click on it.

4. When the auction closes, the auction site will send e-mails to the seller and the highest bidder. These two must figure out the details by themselves in a fixed time frame—usually a week or two. They work out how to pay (check, money order, whatever) and how to deliver— and then follow through on it. Many sellers insist on waiting until out-of-state checks clear before delivery, so the buyer may wait a few weeks after the last bid before seeing the goods.

5. When the goods arrive, it's helpful to leave a feedback message about the experience. Good sellers deserve praise, and other buyers deserve to know if a seller is slow or unpleasant.

now what do I do?
Answers to common questions

How can I avoid shipping costs when returning goods I bought online?

Only a very few companies will cover return shipping costs. But if you're buying from a Web site that's run by a real store, such as Barnes & Noble, you can often return them to the store for in-store credit. Check the site's return and exchange policy before you buy anything, and if this is okay with the company, take the goods and your shipping invoice to the store.

I've had no luck selling stuff at online auctions. What am I doing wrong?

It's easy for sellers to set their opening bids too high and discourage bids. When buyers look for items, they often look not just at the current asking bid but also at the number of buyers who have made bids. The weird thing about auction psychology is that when buyers look at two similar items with identical price tags, the one with more bidders looks like a better deal. For this reason, it's a good idea to open the bidding low. Here's a tip: Before you put your item up, look for other people's auctions for the same item. What's the going rate for this item? What was the starting bid? And is there anything in the description that looks appealing? You shouldn't copy descriptions, but you can learn from other people's sales pitches.

My buddy says you can jack up auctions by logging on under another name and bidding on your own stuff. Is this a good idea?

Absolutely not. It's fraud, for which the Federal Trade Commission slaps on a hefty fine. And it can get you booted off an auction site in a heartbeat. But it's also not a smart tactic because it can backfire too easily, meaning you end up buying your own stuff. Don't consider it.

I don't want to give my credit card number at a Web site. Can I still shop online?

You can, but it'll take a bit more work. Many Web sites have toll-free customer service numbers where you can phone in your credit card number after placing your order. The sales rep will take your credit information and click a button that clears your account at the Web site to make purchases.

A friend sent me an e-mail message with something called Flooz to spend. What is that?

Flooz is an online gift certificate that you can spend at any Web site that takes it. Your buddy used a credit card to give you a line of credit to spend at sites like Tower Records, Godiva Chocolatier, Brookstone, and dozens of other online stores. To spend the Flooz credit, you have to activate it. Click on the link within the e-mail you received and bang! You're ready to spend. To see which sites take Flooz, visit **http://www.flooz.com/spend/** and click on any link that appeals.

My online connection quit half-way through an online purchase order I was making. How can I check whether my order went through or not?

Most online stores send you an e-mail confirming your purchase. So check your e-mail. If there is no message, chances are your purchase didn't go through. Failing that, call their customer service. The phone number should be on their Web page.

When I fill out my address and credit card information, I keep getting error messages. What am I doing wrong?

You probably are forgetting to fill in all the boxes, or you're making a typing error. Many people, for example, forget to type in their phone numbers. Any missing information is usually labeled on the error page. And make sure your credit card information is typed in correctly—some sites want you to put in hyphens, some don't.

 NOW WHERE DO I GO?!

CONTACTS	PUBLICATIONS
Epinions.com **www.epinions.com** Customers post comments about products they have bought and the companies that make them.	**eBay for Dummies** By Roland Werner
	Internet Auctions for Dummies By Greg Holden
Google Directory **directory.google.com/Top/Home/** Click on Consumer Information to find huge lists of helpful sites—including advocacy and price-comparison services.	

CHAPTER 6   GOING PLACES

YOU'RE SITTING IN FRONT OF A COMPUTER—
BUT YOU CAN ALSO BE PLOTTING YOUR ESCAPE
TO A WEEKEND GETAWAY, A LONG VACATION,
OR JUST A TRIP ACROSS TOWN. THE WEB IS
EQUIPPED WITH DOZENS OF SITES FOR THE
NITTY GRITTY OF TRAVEL PLANNING.

GOING PLACES

ROUGH GUIDE **TRAVEL**

▶ HOME ▶ SPOTLIGHT ▶ TRAVEL TALK ▶ INFO ▶ CATALOG ▶ TRAVEL

| Countries | Featured Cities | Complete Ind... |

Indonesia SEARCH

Explore More Than 14,000 Destinations

Southeast **Asia**

Brazil! **Jamaica**

From the Al-Wad Road to Zaragoza, and everything in between.

USE THE PULLDOWN MENUS OR SEARCH TO BEGIN

Rough Guides . . . Smooth Travel
Experience the travel guides online

SPOTLIGHT
On Summer Festivals

The much-loved musical mudbath of Glastonbury may have been called off this year, but there are plenty of events worldwide this summer which offer a big musical buzz, a beautiful setting or just the chance to get down and dirty...
read more

Cool Places

Local Delicacies

▶ Turtle meat, Indonesia

▶ Snake's blood, Thailand

▶ American bison, USA

▶ Witchetty grubs, Australia

MAPBLAST!

1112 21st Ave

San Ramon
San Francisco 680
San Leandro Dublin Livermore
South San Francisco Hayward
Millbrae
San Mateo Fremont
Redwood City 84
101 Milpitas
280 Sunnyvale San Jose
Saratoga Flim Way 87 10 mi

Pacific Ocean

©2001 Vicinity Corp, GDT, NavTech

| Print | Email | Save | Customize | PDA Download | Traffic |

your online travel agent

Plan your next getaway

Many people are happy entrusting their travel plans to a trusted travel agent. But if you aren't among these happy folk, the Web can put you in charge of your own plans. Online trip-planning services give you the power to pick and choose flights, car rentals, and hotel rooms whenever the fancy strikes.

Before you start, you need to know that travel sites will want you to register your name and details before you can get to the good information. You can dabble around as a guest at some sites, but they'll want your information (including credit card details) to book and make reservations. Here are some of the biggest sites to jump-start your travel plans.

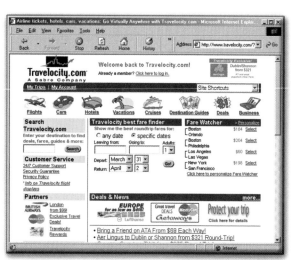

Plan your whole journey from airport to hotel rooms and back again at one-stop travel agent sites such as Travelocity. They give you access to the same database that travel agents use (called Sabre), and a choice of hotels and car rental options.

Expedia (**www.expedia.com**) Microsoft's flight, train, car rental, and hotel booking site includes an online travel accessories shop.

Sidestep (**www.sidestep.com**) This new site searches a vast array of databases to find really competitive prices.

TheTrip (**www.thetrip.com**) This is a good, all-around travel site that is not just for booking travel, cars and hotels, but also for learning about airports, hotels, aircraft and handy traveling skills.

Travelocity (**www.travelocity.com**) This site includes a great inexpensive flight search (if you are a little flexible about your travel time).

TravelWeb (**www.travelweb.com**) TravelWeb's strong suits are its hotel search and weekend-getaway reports. You can restrict your hotel search to hotels with modem lines, free local phone calls and a lot more.

# ASK THE EXPERTS

How do I get tickets if I buy online?

Thanks to computers, airlines don't need to send you paper tickets and boarding passes. Instead, you'll get a confirmation code printed and sent to you on a sheet of letter-sized paper—called an **e-ticket.** You give this to the check-in agent at the airport—along with a photo ID and your credit card for verification.

I have a very tight budget. Are there sites where I can haggle over my ticket cost?

You can name a price you can afford at **Priceline.com**, and wait for airlines to accept your offer. You provide the locations and days you want to travel (and can opt to go a day earlier or later, if you're flexible), then wait 15 minutes for an offer. You enter a binding agreement when you set a fare, so when the offer's made, you're stuck with it. Be aware that you may get no offers at all or be committed to traveling at weird hours with stopovers—but you can save big bucks this way.

Does it matter which site I use?

Your choice of travel site is the same as your choice of travel agent—it's a matter of taste. Shop around before you buy, and see which sites work best for you and give you the information you want. Maybe one site will give you better fares or a better choice of hotels—or you'll just prefer the way it works.

TRAVEL ABROAD

If you're planning a trip abroad, read up on local customs and must-see attractions at international travel sites—from the granddaddy of them all, **Fodors.com**, to younger and hipper sites such as **lonelyplanet.com** and **roughguides.com**. All three sites will tell you about visa requirements, inoculations, and more. To check current news on political instability or epidemics, be sure to check with Uncle Sam—**www.state.gov** provides advisories when you click on Services, then Travel Warnings.

making hotel reservations

Get the best deal in town

Your accommodations can make or break a getaway. The Web can take some of the guesswork out of where to stay. Just check the hotel or lodging link at the travel site you're using. At Travelocity, for example, you enter the days you'd like to stay and the location—within a certain radius of an airport or zip code or famous landmark. You can click in check marks next to must-have options—a gym, child-care facilities, pets allowed—and even state a preference of hotel chains. When you're done, click on the Search Now button, and see what's on the list.

If you don't see any rooms, either lower your standards (do you really need a Jacuzzi in the room?) or check out another travel site to see if they know any better hotels.

Once you get a list of potential hotels to stay at, learn more about the hotels. There will always be a link for more information about the hotel—telling you whether there are premium cable channels in every room, high-speed Internet connections, valet parking, feng shui décor, and a host

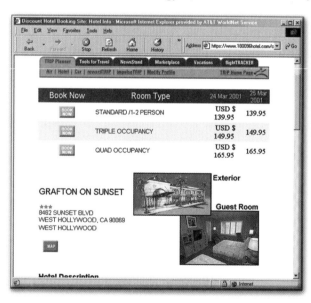

You don't have to rent a hotel room sight unseen. Check out the facilities—and any photographs available—before making your reservation. TheTrip.com and other travel sites provide informational pages on any hotel they give price quotes for.

of other things you may not have thought to ask. You may also see photos of guest rooms and read other details that help you make a final decision. Before you book your room, take a moment and check out the hotels at another site, just to make sure there isn't a better deal somewhere else. For easy comparison shopping have both Web sites open. Here's how: Click on the File menu in the tool bar of the first Web site. Select the New or New Window option. A new Web browser page will open. Type in the address of the other Web site and hit Enter. Both will appear on your screen, one almost on top of the other. Put your mouse anywhere on the partially hidden Web site, which will then take center stage on your screen.

STEP BY STEP: SMART HOTEL STRATEGIES

Sure, you can get a hotel room price quote at **TheTrip.com**, **Expedia.com** or **Travelocity**—but smart travelers check out a hotel's facilities and policies. Is there an on-site restaurant? How near is the hotel to where you're visiting? What's the cancellation policy? Answers to all these things should be available at the booking site. If they're not, pick up a phone and call the number.

1. Get a map Many hotel sites will have links to maps of the surrounding area. If they don't, get their street address, then get over to a map site and figure out directions from there. (Map sites are covered in greater depth on page 113).

2. Check the small print Are there extra charges for extra occupants? Some hotels charge to let the kiddies stay; others don't. What about cancellation charges or surcharges for staying on an extra day because of emergencies?

3. Get with the programs Hotel chains have their own versions of frequent flyer programs. Make sure you're registered with the frequent guest programs of any hotel chain you use, and you may get preferable rates, upgraded rooms or just friendlier service.

renting a car

Find the best deals for your wheels

In their capacity as the travel agents of the Web, travel sites like Expedia, Travelocity and TheTrip can help you to reserve a car of your choice. And they apply the same level of detail to booking cars as they do to reserving flights and hotel rooms. All you have to do is enter the pick-up and drop-off time and date, pick the class of car you want, and the site gives you a price list. There will be links that lead to Web pages that describe the car and the conditions of the rental—including penalties.

Pay close attention to the fine print—the rates quoted on the first results page will not include sales tax, transportation fees, vehicle license fees or other compulsory payments. (Ever heard of "frequent flyer tax recovery surcharge"? You will . . . you will. . . .) If you're on a budget, aim low!

Once again, it's a good idea to shop around—you may find a slightly better deal. And if the travel sites don't provide you with listings for your favorite car rental company, go to the directory at Yahoo, Excite, or Google, and click through the travel sections to car rental.

Get your motor running! Pick the best combination of price and features from the results of a car rental search at a travel site, and you'll be on the highway with the tunes blasting away before you know it.

STEP BY STEP: RENTING A CAR ONLINE

Here's how you'd go about reserving a car rental at the travel site Expedia (**www.expedia.com**). The same principles apply to the other sites, but the details may vary a little.

1. Click on the Cars link on the site's home page.

2. Enter the location and time you want to rent—the pick-up location can be an airport code or a city and state name. Be careful with pick-up and drop-off times—leave yourself with enough time to drop off the vehicle, or you may have to pay for late return.

3. Make a choice from the list of car types—economy, compact, minivan, SUV, and so on. Click on the down-arrow next to the box to see all the contents. And if you have a favorite rental agency, make that selection from a list too.

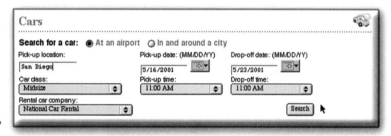

4. When the results of the search come up, look at all the listings—don't immediately click on the cheapest. Make sure that the class of vehicle matches the one you want.

5. Before making a final selection, click on the link that describes the car in question. If the description seems okay, click on Verify Rate and Continue.

6. Check the rate—it may differ from the rate they have on the first results page. The final number you see before you book it is the one you'll pay. And click on the link that shows the taxes and surcharges in the area. States and cities can tack on dollars per day in five or six different taxes. You can't do anything about this and it will affect the price you'll pay.

7. Click on the Continue button, and log in with your Expedia account info. If you don't have an Expedia account, create one from the other link on that page.

getting directions

Directions without having to stop and ask

Logging onto the Internet before a trip beats rolling down a window at a gas station and asking, "How do I get there from here?" And there's a choice of map sites that can give you turn-by-turn directions from point A to point B that you can print out and take with you—or a map of the area surrounding an address or landmark if you prefer, so you can wander off by yourself.

The three biggest map sites online are MapQuest (**www.mapquest.com**), MapBlast (**www.mapblast.com**) and Expedia Maps (**www.expediamaps.com**). All three will give you directions and local maps, but the size of the maps and presentation of the results vary. You'll end up picking one based on your tastes.

FIRST PERSON DISASTER STORY

Price and prejudice

I had a family emergency to deal with on the West Coast, and I had to get there within a week. The airlines were charging thousands of dollars for tickets on such short notice, so I tried naming a price I could afford at Priceline.com. I clicked on as many options as possible, trying to be flexible in hopes of getting my price. When my confirmation e-mail arrived, I was delighted at the price—only $300 and change after taxes. But boy oh boy, was it inconvenient. Two layovers, and I landed at a different airport from the one that's nearest my sister's house. When I arrived—at 11 pm after traveling all day and half the night—my brother, who flew in from New York, told me that he'd gotten a similar ticket price even though he'd specified no more than one layover and been firm about the airport he wanted to land at. I'd just been too flexible.

Mary T., New Castle, Delaware

www.mapblast.com

Mapblast shows its directions in big, clear type, and provides a button that saves the map to your computer or a Palm or other handheld computer. Click once on the map, and it zooms down to a tight detail of the neighborhood with a sliding-scale zoom control. One good feature: You can select options like banks, coffee shops and gas stations from a list, and Mapblast will show the nearest of each on the map.

www.mapquest.com

MapQuest gives lots of options—you can plan a route that avoids toll roads, save directions on a personal Web site and even fax directions from the Web. When you click on the Print link, it provides a clean page with clear directions and two clear maps—and no fussy design. You have two choices of maps. The first shows an overview of the route and a detailed map of the area near your destination; the other shows turn-by-turn maps. Best of all, in some areas, you can click on a link to get live traffic reports. How cool is that?

www.expediamaps.com

When you plan your route, you can opt for the shortest, the quickest or the most scenic route. Expediamaps provides a single overview map of the route with readable directions. If you want more map detail, you have to click on a link to show turn-by-turn maps. You can click on an e-mail link to send directions to friends or family too.

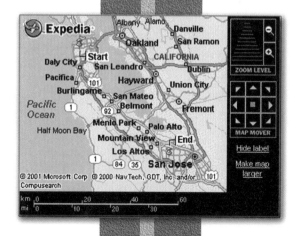

finding entertainment online

What to do if you're new in town

You've checked into a great hotel, with a cool pair of wheels. Now what? Don't stay in and order room service. Get out and enjoy the town. Thanks to the many city guides on the Web, you can find out where to hang out, not to mention cultural events, sports, and all the good shops too.

But what are city guides, and where do you find them, you ask? Well, the major cities get the most extensive coverage (obviously) from the big city-guide sites—Microsoft's **CitySearch**, America Online's **DigitalCity**, and newspaper giant Knight-Ridder's **RealCities**. You can visit any site without having to register, and click on links for pretty much everything from "what's on" guides for the locals to tourist information and area maps.

Want to know what's on in the city you're about to visit? City-guide Web sites such as CitySearch abound—and give you the straight dope on everything you might want to see.

Of course, if you're visiting another country or small-town or rural America, you need another kind of regional site altogether. Try **Yahoo! Get Local**. It's a good starting point—though it's not the only Web directory with a good local listing. Click the Regional link at **Google.com** or Travel at **Excite.com** for great local sites, especially abroad. And when you're researching an area, don't overlook the power of the local media. Find the Web site of the local newspaper and check the current events listings there.

CITYSEARCH
www.citysearch.com
Microsoft's in-depth guide to events, entertainment and landmarks in major U.S. cities is a great starting place. To home in on your city, you use its name in place of the www—as in newyork.citysearch.com.

REALCITIES
www.realcities.com
Owned by a newspaper company, RealCities does a great job of capturing local information for locals and reporting on all the interesting stuff that's going on.

DIGITALCITY
www.digitalcity.com
America Online's big-city guide covers the same ground as the other two big-city sites—and throws in some nice extras, such as the opinions of local experts on places to go.

YAHOO! GET LOCAL
local.yahoo.com
Not interested in big cities? Here's the place to go. Click on the State link and find weather, news and tourist information for more out-of-the-way places. Great if you want to visit Civil War sites in Pennsylvania or hike in central California.

ZAGAT GUIDES
www.zagat.com
If eating out is important, this site condenses some of the more outspoken restaurant diners' reviews known to mankind. You have to sign up for a free registration to read them—but it's worth it.

DINE.COM
www.dine.com
Maybe you don't agree with Zagat. If so, Dine.com lets you see the opinions of lots of different reviewers—you get to judge the judges and make up your own mind by consensus. It's stronger in some regions than others, but Dine.com is a great dining resource.

now what do I do?

Answers to common questions

I prefer to travel by train. Can the Web help me?

Amtrak has a very well developed Web site where you can look up train times, check the facilities on trains and even book tickets. Visit **www.amtrak.com** and click on the link labeled Schedules & Fares or Reservations & Tickets. Enter the locations, dates and times you want to travel for schedules, and click on the results to get sample fares. To reserve tickets, you must register (click on the New Users link) and log in. If you feel like a spontaneous getaway, click on the Special Offers or Rail Sale links on the site's **home page** to check out promotional fares. There are some real bargains posted here from time to time.

Can I find timetables for my local commuter train and bus transit?

The regional transit agencies are different from city to city—the San Francisco Bay Area's BART, New York's MTA and Boston's T are all at different Web sites. You'll probably see your local transit agency's Web address painted on buses and at the rail station. But if you can't remember it, check out the list at a Web site called MetroDynamics (**www.metrodynamics.com/bats/transitagencies.html**) or look up your area at a Web directory or search site.

Is it safe to purchase travel tickets online?

Travel agents have been doing it since before you and I ever could. Airlines and other transportation merchants have had a lot of experience in keeping transactions and personal information secure—so you can rest assured that Travelocity, TheTrip and other travel sites are safe places to do business.

Why are travel sites and mapping sites so slow?

Because they're busy and they are accessing an even busier database. Think of how many people are traveling each day—and how many travel agents and regular Web-surfing joes are buying tickets or checking the maps that enable these jaunts. If you find you're waiting too long, click the Stop button and then click Refresh. If that doesn't work, try visiting another site. There are always other choices that may not be so busy.

What if there's a screwup with my e-ticket?

There really shouldn't be. A lot of people get nervous about going to the airport without a bona fide ticket, but you'll have a confirmation message via e-mail, which you can print out and take with you to the airport if you wish. Otherwise, give the ticket agent your last name, flight number and a photo ID. She will check her computer, find your ticket confirmation and issue you a boarding pass.

Are there any tips for getting a good deal on my airline tickets?

You bet—if you can be a little flexible in your travel times. For starters, try not to travel on the busiest days, namely Monday and Friday. Traveling on a Saturday and returning on a Tuesday or Wednesday can yield the best fares. It's also a good idea to book your flight at least 3 weeks before you fly. Less than 3 weeks and the fares will be up by 60 percent. If possible, consider flying "any time"—it's kind of like flying standby. You tell the travel site the range of days you wish to travel and they book the cheapest price they can find.

NOW WHERE DO I GO?!

CONTACTS	PUBLICATIONS
Tourism Offices Worldwide **www.towd.com**	**Trouble-Free Travel** By Stephen D. Colwell and Ann R. Shulman
National Parks Service **www.nps.gov**	**Packing: Bags to Trunks** By Kim Johnson Gross, Jeff Stone, and Walter Thomas
Fodor's **www.fodors.com**	**Lonely Planet Travel With Children** By Maureen Wheeler
Rough Guides **www.roughguides.com**	**The Penny Pincher's Passport to Luxury Travel** By Joel L. Widzer

WHY DID YOU GET A COMPUTER IN THE FIRST PLACE? TO MAKE YOUR LIFE EASIER, OF COURSE. AND WHAT BETTER PLACE TO START THAN WITH YOUR MONEY? THE INTERNET HAS A GREAT SELECTION OF MONEY-SAVING, STOCK-TRACKING AND STRESS-LOWERING FINANCIAL WEB SITES.

MONEY MATTERS

banking online

Your bank—open 24/7

Tired of traipsing to your ATM to get a balance statement? Fed up with waiting on hold for a bank representative to answer—or worse, waiting on a huge line? Then check into online banking. Many banks offer Web access to their customers. Ask your bank if they offer it, and you may be only an account log-in and password away from checking your balances online. And for simple Web access, you'll rarely be charged a cent. (That's because it's cheaper for a bank to handle simple inquiries over the Net than by phone.)

To get a good idea of the state of the art in online banking, look at **www.cyberinvest.com.** Click on its Banking Center link, and there click on the Guide to Online Banking link. You'll find a table of big national banks that provide online banking services, along with extras they offer, such as links to online brokerages and bill payment.

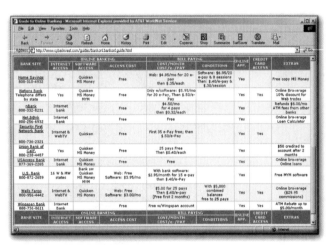

Who's offering online banking? Check out the huge list at Cyberinvest.com. Their online banking guide provides a comparison table of all kinds of features.

Oh, great, you're thinking. Now anybody with a browser may be able to get at my account information. Not so. Banks take security very seriously, and online security is no exception. Banks use secure connections for online banking, which means that everything you see at the Web site and type in there is encrypted (scrambled into code that nobody else can translate). And your information is stored behind a **firewall**, a combination of computers and software that act like the security system at Fort Knox to keep out anyone but authorized people.

SK THE EXPERTS

How much will banks charge me for online banking?

Getting online access to your account with your bank should be free. If you use online banking for paying bills or transferring money to an online brokerage, you may end up paying a monthly flat fee or a charge per transaction—or some combination of the two. These will be direct-debited from your account.

How do I deposit money into an online account?

If you bank online with an insti-tution that doesn't have a branch near you, you have two options. For depositing checks, the bank should supply you postage-paid, addressed envelopes to drop into a mailbox. And for paychecks from your employer, you can arrange for direct deposit using routing num-bers at the bottom of your checks. Direct deposit also makes it easy to wire money to your account. And since it's all online, you can verify any transaction in your Web browser.

How do I get cash?

Ah, there's the rub. You can't print out money using your inkjet printer! To get greenbacks, you'll have to find a real ATM that uses the same system as your bank. The biggest ATM systems nationwide are Cirrus, Plus, MAC and NYCE. Look at the back of your cash card for the logos and match them up to machines in your neighborhood. Take out cash, and your account is posted with a debit notice right away.

financial Web sites

We already know the Web is a rich mine of information—but is it a mine for information about how to get rich? Well, yes it is, up to a point. If you want to pick up information about money management, tax planning, or mutual funds—it's out there. The trick is finding it. So instead of using **search engines,** the librarians of the Web, in a hit-or-miss attempt to track down information, go straight for the money section of any good Web search site or directory. The good stuff is usually sorted into its own channel, with its own short Web address. You'll notice that most of these addresses don't start with www. Don't worry, type them into the Web address section and press Enter—they'll work just the same. Here are five favorites to check out first.

About.com
home.about.com/money

Microsoft
moneycentral.msn.com

Excite
quicken.excite.com

Netscape
personalfinance.netscape.com

Yahoo!
finance.yahoo.com

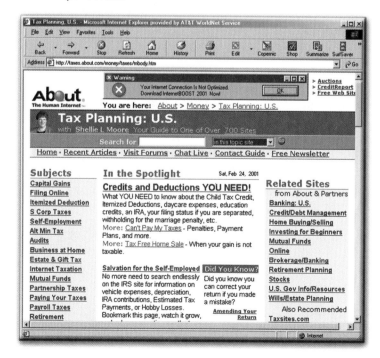

Thinking of money sends you into a panic? Check out About.com. It provides good down-to-earth consumer advice about money sites and money matters.

ASK THE EXPERTS

I'm looking for the best financial research for my investments. Where do I go?

Investment research is a tricky business. Many people sound awfully convincing in this business without actually knowing too much about it. So stick to names you can trust—Bloomberg (**www.bloomberg.com**), Forbes (**www.forbes.com**) and Zacks and the Wall Street Source (which joined forces in an individual investor site at **www.zwss.com**). The good news is that sites like **zwss.com** can provide great authoritative information about thousands of mutual funds, stocks, and more. The bad news is that you can get only one month of free trial time before you have to pony up a monthly fee.

Financial advice seems so general. How can I relate this to my own finances?

Many Web sites include calculators that you can use to enter your real-life figures into a series of little boxes on the screen. When you've entered all the numbers they ask for, you click a button and they will figure out how much money you'll need to retire. You need to enter figures such as your age and income, and estimate your needs down the line, but the calculators handle all the rest. A couple of sites that provide these tools are **www.kiplinger.com** and **www.bloomberg.com**. Try them out—you have nothing to lose.

Can a Web site help me figure out foreign currency?

There is a currency converter that can tell you exactly what the contents of your wallet are worth in yen, euros or UK pounds—and vice versa. It's at **www.xe.com/ucc/** and it's called the Universal Currency Converter. When you get there, type the precise amount to convert in the left-hand box, and locate the currency you're converting from the left-hand list. (The site sorts currency alphabetically by country.) Then in the right-hand list, pick the currency to convert to. Click the button marked Perform Currency Conversion, and bingo! you have the exact current value of those dollars in overseas money.

FINANCIAL NEWS NETWORKS

When you want money news and you want it now, visit these oft-updated sites often.

www.cnbc.com
Breaking news from the cable television channel.

www.cnnfn.com
Another cable network with hot stories about business and the economy.

www.marketwatch.com
The networks are no slouches when it comes to money news—as this CBS site proves.

www.thestreet.com
A trusted source of independent financial news that lives only on the Web.

www.fool.com
Money matters with a down-to-earth attitude from The Motley Fool

paying bills online

Nothing can take all the pain out of paying bills, but the wonderful world of the Web can smooth over some of the biggest problems. If you sign up for electronic payments, you can avoid the mound of paper you wade through and avoid paying late fees.

How does it work? To pay bills online, you send money electronically in an electronic check, which works a bit like a Western Union wire transfer. The check doesn't exist on paper, but it works exactly like a check, right down to the check number.

To start paying bills online, you need to sign up for the service at your bank, or at one of the special Web services that handle payments online. Some institutions charge a monthly fee for the service, others don't if you maintain a certain balance at the bank. For more information, see the table "Take my bills . . . please!" After you're signed up, your credit card, phone company and others will send you e-mail messages to remind you of upcoming bills. You then log on to your bill-paying service—which uses a secure server to keep your finances confidential—and authorize the payments. It takes about 3 days to clear an electronic payment.

If companies that bill you won't take electronic payments, no problem. Your online bank will cut a paper check on your behalf when you authorize payment online, and mail it to whoever wants the cash. You don't even have to know about it. This process takes longer to clear, though—about 5 to 7 days.

ASK THE EXPERTS

What do I need to pay bills online?

You'll need an account at a bank that handles online billing, and you'll need the software that the bank uses to handle transactions. If your local bank branch offers online bill payments, walk in and sign up with their program. If not, or if you think they charge too much, check the online bank listings at **www.cyberinvest.com** or **www.bankrate.com** for the best rates. These comparison sites show you the rates of many online bill-paying services to compare and sign up for online.

What software will I need?

Many banks and other companies provide you with Web-enabled financial software to handle bill paying. Sometimes it's a program you've never heard of, but mostly it's a familiar name such as Quicken or Microsoft Money. Of course, the software is not strictly free, since most companies charge you a little extra for online bill payment (or want you to have a minimum amount in your account to receive the service without extra charges).

online trading

Be your own stockbroker

Instead of paying for a full-service broker to manage a stock portfolio, savvy investors now trade stocks online, using their browser and a secure Web site to handle all transactions. Yes, it is a brave new world, and one you can join too!

Online brokerages enable their members to bid on, buy and sell securities (stocks, bonds and so on) using a Web browser—in addition to checking the value of their portfolios in a table that updates as the market moves. Sure, you still pay commissions, but they are a fraction of what you would have to pay some guy in an expensive suit, and you have more control over the process.

To begin your online trading career, first scrape together the money to fund your account. Most brokerages require a minimum amount, which could be $5,000 or less. Then find a brokerage that suits you. There are plenty actively trading over the Internet, including Ameritrade (**www.ameritrade.com**), Datek Online (**www.datek.com**), E-Trade (**www.etrade.com**), Charles Schwab (**www.schwab.com**) and Fidelity Investments (**www.fidelity.com**).

Once you've picked a brokerage, you pick an account. They're broadly divided into individual, joint (for yourself and a spouse), professional (for businesses) and retirement (IRA) accounts. You will be asked to provide personal data, including your social security number. (It's okay to do this over a secure connection—but don't give this stuff out to anyone else, okay?) Once you've filled out all this stuff, you must sign and return several agreement forms, and deposit funds in the account.

Then you'll be given a user ID and password to log on to your account. With funds in your account, you're ready to trade.

STEP BY STEP: HOW TO PICK AN ONLINE BROKER

1. First, find out who's out there. The Motley Fool (**www.fool.com**) has a terrific comparison table of online brokers.

2. How much do they want up front? Rule out the brokers who want a minimum deposit that's higher than you can afford.

3. Find the hidden charges. Commission charged per trade varies from extreme discount houses which charge $7 to $12 per trade, to midprice at $12 to $20, and high-price brokers who think that $30 is reasonable. But don't stop there—scour the small print for surcharges (fees for transferring money into or out of your account, account inactivity fees, annual fees, and fees for not maintaining a minimum balance).

4. What services do they offer? A wide range of investment vehicles is good, but don't underestimate the value of old-fashioned service. On the Web, that means an easy-to-use Web site that responds quickly. It means phone numbers, preferably toll-free, to call with queries. (Test their response time with a call before committing your life savings to their service.)

5. Don't scrimp. If you're only making less than twenty trades a year, then saving ten bucks on a trade should not be a big priority. Look for a brokerage that offers good customer service. A hundred bucks extra in fees for great advice and great service is a sound investment.

buying and selling a house online

Serious shopping online

It's incredible. You can use the Web to buy or sell a house anywhere in the States—and in many other places in the world. The Internet's ability to combine pictures with descriptive text makes it an ideal aid in the arduous task of buying or selling a house.

Start with where you want to live. Enter the zip code or town name of a place you're considering at one of the following sites—

Realtor.com or **HomeAdvisor.com**. There you can find statistics about key factors such as schools (including test results, class sizes, etc.), crime statistics, and neighborhood businesses. Real estate sites also provide demographic information such as median household income and the number of single-family homes there are in an area.

Once you've settled on a neighborhood, you can stay with those sites and check listings by price range or facilities. Or you can use any of the realtor sites—

Homeseekers.com, **Realtor.com**, and **Homeadvisor.com**—in your quest. If you absolutely have to have 5 bedrooms and 7 bathrooms in the 90210 zip code, then enter those figures in the boxes labeled Bed, Bath and Zip, and anything that matches will turn up. Many houses in the list won't have addresses—instead you're given the local realtor's contact info—but you'll get a good idea of what's available. And there's a quick estimator of your mortgate payments at a standard 15- or 30-year mortgage. Just be aware that you'll need to factor in taxes and closing costs separately

Most real estate sites will put you in touch with local realtors if you like, or provide you with e-mail alerts whenever a likely house comes on the market. If you are in the market for a house, check all the sites, as some sites have exclusive listings.

ⒶSK THE EXPERTS

How much house I can really afford?

You know roughly how much money you make and how much you have. Feed that information into a financial calculator at a good real estate site. HomeFair at **homefair.com** has a particularly good set of calculators that enable you to figure out what you can afford.

I'm relocating out of state. How do I get started?

Homefair.com (which is a subset of **Realtor.com**) provides all kinds of useful information, ranging from cost of living comparisons to budget advice for moving costs. Enter your current address and the place you're moving to, and you'll get an idea of how much further your dollar will go in the new place. And with the tips you get about dealing with movers, you should be able to save a little on those costs too.

I'm selling my house. How do I get it on the Web?

Traditionally, when you sell a house, the agent advertises the property in newspapers and in personal referrals. The agent also shares the information with other agents to see if they can sell it for him. If the property is actually sold by another agent, the listing agent gets a cut of the fee. That's the traditional route—and the Web works in a similar way. Real estate Web sites get a cut of property sales they refer to other agents. If you want to get your property listed on these real estate Web sites, you need to list your house with an agent who's hooked in to one of those sites. Or if you're selling the property yourself, check out the sites yourself and see what it takes to sign up as a seller. (Be warned—not every real estate site deals directly with sellers).

REAL ESTATE SITES

Get a feel for the housing market in your area (or another one, if you can relocate), by visiting several of these sites.

www.realtor.com
Listings of 1.4 million homes from more than 5,000 listing services are impressive enough, but Realtor.com has more up its sleeve, including great relocation information and financial calculators.

www.homeadvisor.com
Microsoft's HomeAdvisor site provides great profiles of neighborhoods, especially the demographic breakdown of inhabitants. Its listings are good too.

www.homeseekers.com
With daily updates, these listings of residential and commercial properties are worth a close look.

www.homebuilders.com
If you plan to build a new home, find one of 125,000 builder listings here.

now what do I do?
Answers to common questions

Can hackers eavesdrop on my visits to an online bank?

Hackers can't break into a secure connection between your PC and a Web site. How do you know if your connection's secure? Look at the Web address in your browser. Usually, a Web address begins with http://, but when you get to the page where you enter personal data, such as your bank account numbers, there should be https://. The "s" stands for secure, so that's how you can feel about your transaction. Another way to tell that you have a safe connection is a padlock icon at the bottom of your browser's window. See a closed padlock in the bar at the bottom? That's secure too. An open or broken padlock isn't.

Can I trust a mortgage site to give me the best rates?

Most mortgage sites are operated by mortgage agencies that ideally will give you the best deal. Some let you prequalify for a loan, such as **www.eloan.com** and **www.homeadvisor.com**. Others such as **www.mortgagelocator.com** help you find interested lenders. If you are looking for independent mortgage advice, try **www.hsh.com**.

How can I get a better loan rate than the one I'm being offered?

Put your business up for bid! If you have a quote in hand and you want a better deal, visit **Priceline.com**, a Web-based service that lets you drive a hard bargain. You type in the terms you're interested in for a home mortgage, refinancing or equity loan. Within six business days, one of the participating lenders will meet your terms—or the deal's off and you must reapply. This is not a service for tire kickers, though—you must commit to a good-faith deposit of $200 when a lender makes an offer, so make sure in advance that it's something you really want.

I need a credit card, but I want a good deal. Can the Web help?

You bet! Many banking and finance Web sites will advertise their special credit card. But if you care more about a good rate than having a card with Yahoo! printed on it, visit a rate-comparison site. Credit Card Search Engine (**www.creditcardsearchengine.com**) is one good place to start.

I can't even think about investments until I sort out my monthly bills. Any help available online?

Odd you should ask. There's one site that focuses on reducing monthly bills—whether it's for phone service, cell phones, utilities or credit card balances. It's even got an easy-to-remember name—**LowerMyBills.com**. Instead of picking phone companies based on guesswork and slick marketing, go to this site to see the best deals in your area. They're updated regularly. Reducing your outgoing money is the first step in having money to invest . . . so try it out.

How do I find the current interest rate?

Several banking sites provide prominent daily updates for mortgage rates, as well as rates for CDs and money markets. Try **www.banxquote.com** or **www.bankrate.com**.

 OW WHERE DO I GO?!

CONTACTS	PUBLICATIONS
Online Banking Report A periodical that's been reporting on the online banking industry since 1995. **www.onlinebankingreport.com** **U.S. Treasury** Tax help and information from Uncle Sam's piggy bank **www.ustreas.gov**	**Banking Online for Dummies** By Paul A. Murphy **The Online Banking Newsletter** 800-732-8104

CHAPTER 8 YOUR OWN WEB PAGE

WANT TO HAVE YOUR OWN WEB PAGES?
IMPOSSIBLE, YOU CRY? WITH A LITTLE KNOWL-
EDGE AND A LITTLE CLICKING, IT'S DO-ABLE.
READ ON AND SEE HOW TO CREATE YOUR OWN
WEB PAGE IN CYBERLAND.

what is a Web page?

Revealing the code
behind the pages
you browse

Web pages are the "pages" you see when you surf the Net and
stop at a site. Usually, they contain text with graphics—photos, spot
art, illustrations, you name it. Web pages may look like regular
documents with text and a photo or two—the kind you can create
in any word processing program—but they are different creatures.

Web pages contain two types of text—words you see on the screen,
and hidden codes behind those words that tell your browser software how to show the words and graphics. These codes (written in
HTML, a computer language for the Web) do all kinds of things,
such as set the color of the background and the text, scale the text
to a particular size and tell the browser which pictures to show at
what size.

Computer code? Don't panic. The small amount you need to know
is right here in this chapter. But if you want a Web page and can't
bear the idea of creating it yourself, hire a techy teenager to create
one for you. It shouldn't take more than an hour.

Why have a Web page, you ask? Well, aside from the fun of it all,
Web pages can be very useful. Consider these: A Web page for your
daughter's upcoming wedding that gives guests all the necessary
information about hotels, ceremony directions, etc. Or a Web page
on your club's big fund-raising event, informing the public of where
and when (and yes, you can put that Web address in the local
newspaper too). Or if your family is scattered all over the globe, a
Web page devoted to family milestones and pictures.

What a Web browser shows

To your Web browser, these pages are identical. It shows you the pretty one (top), while keeping hidden the codes that created it (below).

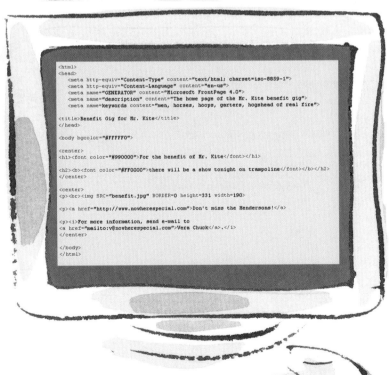

What a Web browser sees

Computer code tags are easy to spot—they are enclosed in angle brackets. For example, a tag that begins body copy would look like this: <body>. A tag with a backslash signals the end of the copy: </body>.

getting started

What, me?
Design a Web page?
Yes, you can!

Fortunately, there are Web design programs that not only let you bypass all the computer code stuff but are free. The two most popular Web design programs are Microsoft FrontPage Express and Netscape Composer. If you have Microsoft Office (version 97 or 2000) or Netscape Communicator 4.0, you'll already have one of these Web design programs. You can find them under the Start menu in Programs. If you don't, you can download either of them free of charge. See page 69.

STEP BY STEP: CREATING YOUR OWN WEB PAGE

1. Open Netscape Composer or Microsoft Front Page. It will open to a blank page, pretty much as a word processor does.

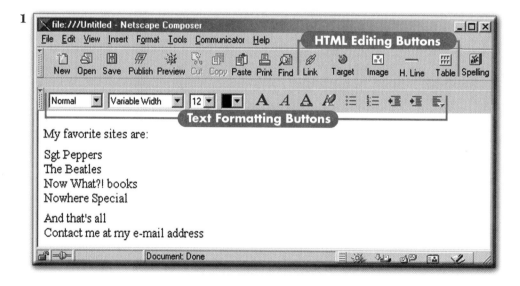

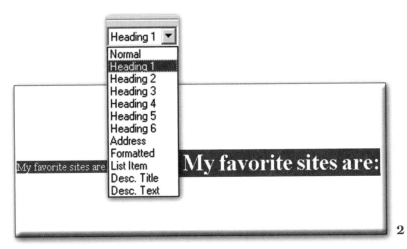

2

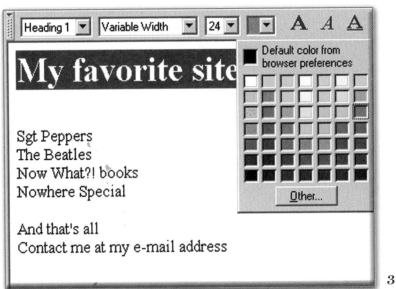

3

2. Type what you want in your Web page into a window.

3. Now you need to **format** (or position) your words so they appear in the right place. Web pages have pretty simple text formats—a large headline is called Heading 1, a slightly smaller one is Heading 2 and so on. To format text, first drag the mouse across the text in question to highlight it, then go to the text formatting toolbar and find the list for the type of text you want. You can also change the font to one you like better, and even change the text color if you like.

getting started,

4. After you've done a little editing, select the File menu and click on Save or Save As. The first time you do this, type in index.html or default.html. (For all subsequent Web pages, you can call it anything you want, just no spaces in the title.)

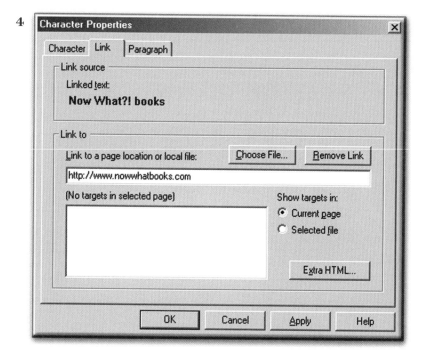

5. Add **links** (underlined words that if clicked will automatically link readers to relevant sites). First click and drag your mouse across the word you want to link to a Web site. Then click on the Link button in the toolbar. In the dialog box, type in the Web address of a site you know. You must enter the http:// before any Web address. For example, to link to the Web site for Now What?! Books, you'd type in http://www.nowwhatbooks.com without any spaces or extra punctuation.

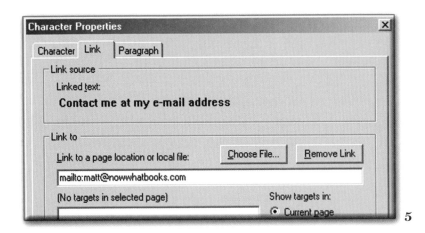

5

6. Add e-mail links. This lets your readers send you e-mail effortlessly. First, type in the text, such as "Contact me at my e-mail address," then highlight the text, then click on the Links button. Next, type in your e-mail address. To create an e-mail link to Matt at Now What?! Books, for example, you'd type mailto:matt@nowwhatbooks.com without any spaces or extra punctuation.

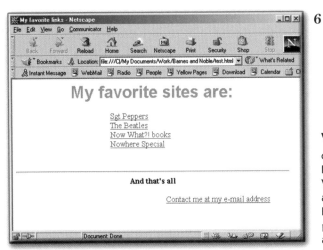

6

When viewers click on the the underlined words in your Web page, they will automatically be linked to other web pages or your e-mail address.

7. Check your work. After you've saved your page, open it in a Web browser and see how it looks. Click on any links you've made too—check that they open the Web page you thought they would.

Hey! Well done! You've just made a Web page.

adding graphics

Jazz up your Web page with a little art

If your Web pages lack that oomph that you see on other people's sites, add some **graphics** (spot art consisting of photos or drawings). Where to get graphics? Web-hosting sites such as the one from your service provider or Homestead usually provide some useful spot illustrations. And you can use free clip art from other sites, such as **www.clipart.com**, that provide pictures free of charge. See Step by Step for how.

If you want your Web site to really stand out, join the Web hosting sites of Homestead or GeoCities. They have wonderful Web-building tools that are available to members. The best thing about these Web sites is that they offer a wide range of **templates,** or ready-made designs for whole Web sites, including links to visit other pages on the site. You simply pick a look you like and type in your own words in place of "dummy" text. When you click the Finish or Publish button at the bottom of the page, your ready-made Web site appears online. You can go back and edit the pages later.

STEP BY STEP: DOWNLOADING

1. Click on the image you want to download, and the File Download dialogue box appears.

2. Click the Save this Program to Disk option and click the OK button.

3. Then indicate where you want to save the file on your hard drive and click the Save button. You will then see a dialogue box giving you the download information—that is, how the download is going, how long it will take and when it is complete. (The faster your modem, the faster it will be to download images.)

4. To insert the picture you've downloaded from the Web, first open up the document you want and click in the text where you want it to go. Next, go up to the Menu bar and click Insert. Go down to Picture and hold, go to From File and click. Find the file that contains your picture and click on it. Go back up to the Menu bar and click on Insert, and presto! Your picture should be in your document.

FORMAT AND FUNCTION

GIF (which stands for graphic interchange format) is most often used for pictures with few colors in them—buttons, cartoons and other illustrations. JPEG files are for photographs—the format takes its name from the consortium that developed it, the Joint Photographic Experts Group. You may also find BMP (bitmap) files online, but they are comparatively large files, so it's best to use GIFs and JPEGs.

ASK THE EXPERTS

What happens if I get disconnected during the download?
If you have any problems when downloading files, such as getting disconnected, or if you accidentally click the Cancel button, simply try the download again.

What if I am asked for my credit card number?
If the Web site specifies that you need to purchase a file before you download it, you might be asked to give your credit card number. Make sure you are on a secure page before you type in your credit card number. If there is a little padlock icon at the bottom of your browser window screen, it is secure.

scanning pictures

Put a photo of your family on your Web page

Want to insert pictures of the kids? Your scorecard from the time you broke 100 on the golf course? That adorable smile of your first grandchild? It's easy to do with something called a scanner, a device that looks a lot like a home photocopy machine. A scanner will copy your picture electronically, meaning that it converts it into a computer file that you can store in your computer. How exactly is it done? Well, after the image is placed on the scanner surface and the light hits or passes through it, the image is converted into computer code and stored as a digital file in your computer. Computer folk refer to this image as the scanned image.

There are many different types of scanners, but flatbed scanners are the best for home use, and the least expensive. You can buy a scanner at most computer stores. Scanners scan whatever you want, color or black and white. Key point: You can print out a color picture only if you have a color printer; if you have a monochrome printer (techspeak for black and white), your color picture will print out in black and white.

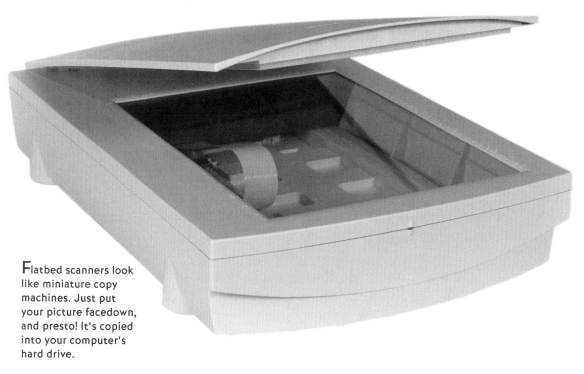

Flatbed scanners look like miniature copy machines. Just put your picture facedown, and presto! It's copied into your computer's hard drive.

STEP BY STEP: SCANNING

1. Turn on the scanner.

2. Turn on your computer.

3. Raise the scanner lid. Place the picture to be scanned facedown on the glass and close the lid. Take care not to scratch the glass.

4. Open the scanner software application on your computer. This assumes that you have already installed the software.

5. Tell the scanner what type of original art you are scanning by choosing reflective for photographs or transparency for slides.

6. Choose a Mode by selecting grayscale or color.

7. Choose a resolution: 72 dpi (low resolution, minimum detail, good for posting to the Web), 150-300 dpi (better detail, but the larger file takes more time to open on the Web).

8. Choose a size: 100 percent is the default.

9. Click Preview. If you like what you see, click Scan.

10. Click Save. You will be asked to choose a file format (don't worry—we'll explain this) and the destination, usually a folder on your hard drive.

Now a quick word about file formats—a technical term for how the art is stored. Your computer will offer you a lot of formats to choose from, but the best choice is JPEG for photographs and GIF for other color graphics. That's because most Windows programs and Web browsers can open these formats—and that's the important thing. And don't waste a minute wondering what those terms mean!

your photos on the Web

Get your photos developed online

You don't have to stick with off-the-shelf pictures on your Web pages. One of the great things about personal Web pages is that you can put personal pictures on them too. There are several ways of doing this—just pick a couple that look good from this list and try them out. Once you have your photos on your computer hard disk, you can incorporate them into your Web pages using your Web page software.

Online Film Development   If you have a regular camera that uses regular film, you can develop computer files as well as prints. When you finish a roll, check out Kodak's **Photonet.com** or **Snapfish.com** for their development deals. They can provide prints and digital photos that you can download from a secure password-protected Web site. Some real life stores with photo development services will also give you photos on disk or on CD for a few extra bucks.

Digital Cameras   It looks and works like a regular camera, but a digital camera contains no film—just a computer memory card and batteries. You plug a digital camera into your computer using a serial or USB (universal serial bus) cable, and use software to take the pictures off the camera and onto your hard disk.

FIRST PERSON   DISASTER STORY

Pretty pictures in a row

I was amazed at how easy it is to save pictures from Web sites—I often right-click on pictures and save them to my hard disk. I saved a couple of great photographs that way that I later put into my Web page. Imagine my surprise when I got an e-mail message from a law firm telling me I was breaking the law! It turned out that the photographer who posted these pictures to his Web site was exercising his rights under copyright law . . . and that I was not allowed to use the pictures. Sure enough, when I checked with my brother-in-law the lawyer, I found out that you are not permitted to take and reuse anything from any Web site unless the site specifically says you can. After the surprise of getting that e-mail message, I will borrow more carefully next time.

Will G., Boston, Massachusetts

SK THE EXPERTS

My digital camera's pictures are too big for my Web page. What can I do?

Most digital cameras have three settings—low, medium and high resolution. The highest resolution pictures are measured in megapixels, meaning that they have at least a million pixels or dots in them. This means that they take up a lot of screen size—and a lot of kilobytes of disk space too. Use low or medium sized pictures for pictures you'll use on your Web site. And use your camera's photo-editing software to crop out anything you don't need to show. Why? Because an oversized, slow-to-load photograph won't work on a Web page as well as a three-inch-square, fast-loading picture.

Where can I find out more about digital cameras?

Like all computer technology, digital photography gets better and less expensive every year. Before you shell out for a digital camera (which will cost at least $100 at current prices), research what's best at a reputable consumer electronics site like **www.pcphotoreview.com** or **MySimon.com**.

Is a digital camera the same thing as a Web cam?

Not exactly. Both take pictures of the real world and turn what they see into a computer graphics file. But a digital camera is something you can carry around in your pocket and point-and-click at whatever you like. A Web cam is more like a closed-circuit television camera—it's a video camera that is wired to a computer, and whatever it's viewing is accessible online via an Internet address. When you type in a Web cam's address, you can see what the camera is viewing. That's how people view live events, such as concerts and interviews, online.

getting a
Web site online

**I've got
a Web page...
now what do I do
with it?**

Now that you've created your very own Web page, you need to put it up on the Internet. To do that, you need to find a **Web host** (a powerful computer that is permanently hooked up to the Internet). Your Internet Service Provider may be able to act as your Web host. America Online, CompuServe, and MSN Internet Access provide Web hosting. (In fact, these services do more than just host Web sites—they also provide Web page forms that walk you through building your own Web pages right there on the Web. So when you're done making the Web page, it's already on the Web!)

If your Internet Service Provider doesn't offer hosting for Web sites, don't worry. Lots of enterprising companies have built up whole communities around their Web hosting. Here is a list of them. They're all free (if you don't mind their putting an ad or two on your Web page to pay the bills):

www.homestead.com

angelfire.lycos.com, www.tripod.com

geocities.yahoo.com

http://www.nbci.com/mywebsite

registering your Web page

Buy a name for your Web page

Great—you've done it! You've actually made your own Web page and got it on the Internet. Wow! The only problem is that your friends keep forgetting the mile-long Web address they have to type in to find it. If you want to make it easy to find your Web page, you can buy a name for your Web page, one that ends in .com or .org or .net. This is called registering your own **domain** (a geek word for the Internet's address system). Consider how much easier it is to type in www.nowherespecial.com, for example, instead of www.angelfire.com/members/nowherespecial/default.html.

The downside is that you have to pay for the privilege, and it's a recurring payment. Depending on where you register your domain, it can cost between $10 and $40 a year—or more if you want more features, such as e-mail addresses.

Where do you register domains? There are literally dozens of sites accredited by the Internet governing body to do this, and hundreds of companies that resell the services under their own brand names. This makes the choice confusing unless you go to a good buyers' guide site. Two sites that make independent comparisons of domain registrars are RegSelect (**www.regselect.com**) and Domain Buyers Guide (**www.domainbuyersguide.com**). Both lists lots of places you can register your domain, and list pros and cons for each place.

MASTER OF YOUR DOMAIN

Here are four sites that can register your domain name (that's a Web address, like your domain-name.com) for you. There are more than 50 other sites where you can do this.

Dotster.com	NameZero
www.dotster.com	**www.namezero.com**
Domain Direct	Register.com
www.domaindirect.com	**www.register.com**

now what do I do?

Answers to common questions

People are saying my Web site is too slow to open. What can I do to speed things up?

Experts in Web design say that if a Web page takes more than ten or fifteen seconds to open, visitors will lose interest really fast. So what makes a Web site slow? The biggest culprit is pictures. A full-screen photograph can be a megabyte in size and take more than a minute to open on a dial-up Internet connection. The same picture at a quarter screen will load much faster and also allow more space on-screen for captions and other Web site information. So use the program that comes with your digital camera or some other graphics software program to resize images. Another problem is putting too much text on one page. If a page seems to load slowly, break it in half and make a new page—then put a "continued" link at the bottom of the first page to take you to the second.

How do I add a second or third page to my Web page?

It's pretty easy, really. First of all, you make a second Web page in the same way as you made the first . . . then you make a third, fourth, and so on. Then you add links to your first Web page—your home page, as it's called in the biz—that people can click to visit your new pages. This process is easiest at Web hosts like Homestead and Tripod, which have page designs with the links already made for you. But even if you're making your pages by hand, it's not tough. When you've made a page, save it with a file name you'll remember (page2.html, page3.html, and so on, are easy). Then you open the home page (which is called index.html or default.html, remember?) and add a link that goes straight to page2.html. To add a link, you first write on the home page a line that says "Click here for page 2," then select that line and click on the Link button, and a blank insert box will appear. Type in the file name "page2.html" in the Insert Hyperlink box and close it. You're done.

How do I update my Web page?

This is a cinch. In your Web page software or at your Web-hosting site, click on the name of the file you want to update. (If it's the home page, it's called index.html or default.html.) When it opens, you then make whatever changes you need to make to the contents of the page. Then you save it with the same name, and voila, your page is updated. If you did this while at your Web-hosting site, it would automatically be uploaded onto the Web. If you updated the page on your hard disk, you need to resubmit it to your Web host.

I used a referral site to index my Web page to all the search engines, but it's still not coming up. Why not?

Chances are your Web page doesn't have any useful key words or descriptions that would allow it to be accessed by a search engine. How do you improve on that? You need to supply better meta tags. Ah, welcome to the really geeky world of Web page wizardry. **Meta tags** are bits of HTML code that Web browsers can read, but which don't show on your Web page. They're important to search engines because they use meta tags to decide which Web sites are the best match for the key words that Web searchers enter. There are two important types of meta tag—keywords and descriptions—which you should enter at the top of your Web pages. Here's how they might look:

<meta name="description" content="grandchildren on your knee">

<meta name="keywords" content="Vera, Chuck, Dave">

In this example, you'd expect to find Dave's Web page somewhere in the results of a Web search for "grandchildren Vera and Dave."

OW WHERE DO I GO?!

CONTACTS	PUBLICATIONS
User Interface Engineering Reports **http://www.uiereports.com**	**Designing Web Usability: The Practice of Simplicity** By Jakob Nielsen
WebWord **http://www.webword.com**	**I just bought a Digital Camera, Now What?!** By Dave Johnson
Web Pages That Suck **http://www.webpagesthatsuck.com**	
Builder.com **www.builder.com**	**Creating Killer Web Sites** By David Siegel

CHAPTER 9 THAT'S ENTERTAINMENT

IT'S ALL SINGING, ALL DANCING, ROUND-THE-CLOCK FUN. NO, REALLY . . . THE WEB IS FULL OF GREAT WAYS TO PASS THE TIME. IT MAY NOT BE AS SLICK AS TV, BUT IF YOU'RE UP FOR A LITTLE FUN ON DEMAND, THE WEB'S THE PLACE TO GO FOR IT.

THAT'S ENTERTAINMENT

get plugged in

You, your Web connection, and a couple of pieces of free software...

You can't play tennis without a racket, and you can't play music or watch movies on the Internet without the right software. You can add all-singing, all-dancing programs with ease. These special software programs are called **plug-ins**, and they turn your computer into a virtual VCR for playing movies, a radio set for playing special Internet-only radio programs, and a music center for recorded music.

Music and sound plug-ins There are two kinds of sound on the Internet—sound files that you download and then listen to, and sound that streams across the wires and gets played as it arrives—a bit like the way radio works. For downloadable audio files, Windows users can use Microsoft's Media Player (it's probably already installed on your computer—check under the Start menu's Programs option—it should be in the list there). A good alternative is a free download program called WinAmp, and for Mac users, MacAmp.

With the right plug-in program such as this one, RealPlayer, you can watch videos, play music, and listen to virtual radio programs, all over the Internet

For those radio-style streaming audio files, RealAudio format is the standard. RealNetworks' RealPlayer is the program that plays these files—and it also handles lots of other formats too, including Windows Media files. RealPlayer also provides "tuning" to various Internet "radio stations" (that is, links to sites that provide RealAudio streaming sounds). RealPlayer plays on Windows and Mac OS computers, plus lots of different Unix workstations too.

Video plug-ins Like sound, video on the Internet comes either as a downloadable file or in streaming format. There are two popular downloadable video players—Apple's QuickTime and Microsoft's Windows Media Player—each of which handles a different format of video file. They can both contain the same kind of movie, but each needs a special kind of player. For streaming video, Media Player handles the Windows Media format (naturally enough). For the more popular RealVideo format, you'll need RealPlayer (yep, the same program that plays RealAudio files).

Animation and games   Visit sites run by big-time broadcasters such as CNN, Comedy Central, and Disney and you'll find cool-looking animations and interactive three-dimensional games—but only if you have a special animation plug-in installed. Two animation plug-ins have pretty much cornered this market—Flash and Shockwave—both developed by animation company Macromedia. Both programs run on Windows and the MacOS, so all home computer buffs can experience the fun.

 SK THE EXPERTS

Where do I find the download sites for plug-ins?

You can go to the individual sites—such as **www.macromedia.com** for Flash and Shockwave, **quicktime.apple.com** for QuickTime player, and **www.real.com** for RealPlayer. Or you can check out sites that list all the plug-ins you could possibly want—such as **www.plugins.com** (click on the Browser link for all the browser plug-ins). The choice is yours.

How do I download and install a plug-in?

Flash and Shockwave are the easiest programs to install—when you go to a site that has a Flash or Shockwave game, it will offer to install the program right away. Just follow the instructions and you'll be ready in no time. The other programs are a little trickier—you'll usually have to fill in your e-mail address and maybe your zip code and some other details, and then click a Download button. When the program's on your hard disk, you must find it, double-click on it, and install it like any other program.

finding music

Get down to the funky rhythm... or get downloading it, at least

The Web is alive with the sound of music, but it's really digital music and it comes in different formats.

Just as regular music might be recorded on cassette, CD, or even vinyl record (to say nothing of 8-tracks and reel-to-reel), digital music that you can download can be in different file formats. The most popular format by far is **MP3**, because it's pretty small and sounds pretty good. Another file format with a growing following is Windows Media Audio (**WMA**), which is a little more compact than MP3. You'll see both formats at music download sites.

Can't find a song you're looking for at MP3.com? Look at eMusic.com, which lets you download songs for dollars (or just cents).

You can find songs in both formats at several sites. **MP3.com** is the best known (with a Web address like that, it's hardly surprising), but other sites also do a bang-up job, including eMusic (**www.emusic.com**) and Napster (**www.napster.com**).

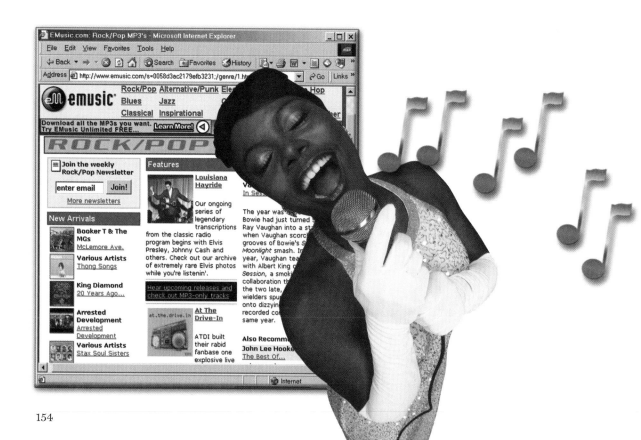

Lately, the recording industry has worked hard to introduce digital file formats with security measures built in that make them difficult to pirate. The two big formats are Windows Media Audio and Liquid Audio. If you go to big commercial sites such as Tower Records or Virgin's JamCast, you'll find files for sale in these formats. They're kind of expensive at a buck or two a song, and they aren't easy to copy from your computer to other devices.

ⒶSK THE EXPERTS

I thought downloading digital music from MP3.com and napster.com was against the law. Will I get into trouble playing them?

Digital music, like music on CDs, is protected by copyright law. But there's nothing illegal or immoral about downloading any digital music as long as the copyright holder allows it. Most artists and record companies, however, allow it only if you pay a small fee when you download their music.

watching videos

You supply the popcorn

Got a couple of hours to spare—or just a couple of minutes? Either time slot is just about enough to take in a movie on your computer. Whether your tastes run to rock videos, experimental animation or Oscar-winning short films, you can find them socked away on Web sites somewhere. If you're equipped with RealPlayer, Windows Media Player, or Apple's QuickTime player, you have the virtual VCR you need to play the movie.

It's possible to stumble upon movie clips and trailers at the Web sites of TV, record and movie companies, but it's more efficient to visit a showcase site. If you open the RealPlayer or Windows Media Player, you'll see buttons labeled Channels or Media Guide. These lead to Web sites that show off the kind of movies you can watch with these two players. Microsoft's Media Guide (**http://windowsmedia.com/mediaguide**) showcases everything from Lenny Kravitz videos to movies—drawing on some excellent sites across the Web. It's a good place to sample the goods and find content sites that deliver what you want to watch. The same applies to Real's site (**http://realguide.real.com**), which also prominently features Web-casts (the online equivalent of broadcasts) of sports events.

Be warned though: Web movies appear in very small screens, and they can look pretty blurry. This is because, unlike cable television, the Internet cables don't have much capacity to spare. Keep your eyes open in the years to come, though—this technology will advance at an impressive rate!

SK THE EXPERTS

Next to the movies I want to watch, I see three links— 28K, 56K, and 112K. What do they mean?

When moviemakers prepare their videos for the Internet, they usually make several versions for different connection speeds. 28K works best for a 28 Kbps modem, 56K for a 56 Kbps modem, and 112K for a cable or DSL connection. In general, you should click the link with the number that matches your connection speed, because the lower numbers have lower picture quality. But don't click a link that's higher than your connection speed—this means that the video files are much bigger, and the Web won't be able to get them to your computer fast enough to watch.

This video looks more like a slide show. What's happening?

The problem's a common one. Like all movies, Web movies are based on a trick of the eye. You think you see pictures moving, but you're actually seeing a sequence of pictures with slight differences (movie types call these pictures frames). Over the Web, however, the movies can drop frames because of busy Internet lines. So sometimes you see a virtual slide show instead of something that looks like a movie. But don't fret—it can usually be fixed. Try closing your player software and clicking on the next lowest connection speed—that is, if you have a 56Kbps modem, click to view the 28K movie. Because the smaller numbers mean smaller video files, the Web should be able to deliver more frames per second—which means more movement. Also, don't try to download anything while you are watching a video. That can distort your viewing.

Web cams

Around the world in eighty digital cameras

Armchair travel is one of the great luxuries of the modern age. Instead of beating a path with machetes through the jungles of Borneo, we can sit on a couch with a remote control and flip channels to a wide variety of nature and travel shows. But for the ultimate in reality television, you can't beat a Web cam.

Physically, Web cams are just like closed-circuit television cameras plugged into a computer. They cost less than a hundred dollars, and many people stick them on top of their computers to add live pictures of themselves for Web chatting. (See pages 166-169 for more about chatting online.) But about a decade ago, computer scientists started pointing them at things that interested them—coffee machines in the break room, traffic on area bridges and scenic views that would give them a break from the cubicles they worked in. A whole new culture of armchair travel began—with live pictures of real events, delivered over the Internet.

Most Web cams show still pictures right there in your browser, in the Web-friendly JPEG picture format, and refresh the picture every few minutes. Some provide full-on moving video pictures using a browser plug-in such as RealPlayer. In each case, you'll see events roughly as they happen—without sound and sometimes in a slide-show format. But what you see in the cam windows varies widely. Radio and television stations love to lace their Web sites with traffic and scenic cams of their local area—and provide a service for commuters in windowless cubicles in the process. Zoos and museums like to show off their exhibits too.

Take a real live look at a shark in Boston's New England Aquarium, or check out the spots on the sun.

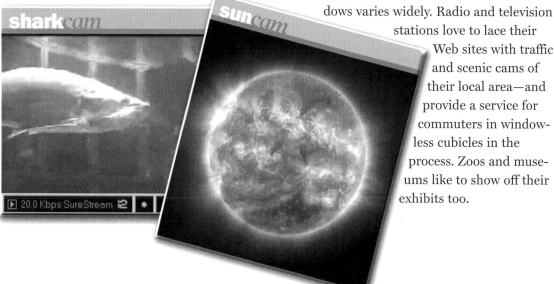

shark**cam**

▶ 20.0 Kbps SureStream

sun**cam**

Here are some possible leads for cams that might interest you. Since cams come and go, it's better to look up current lists at cam directory sites than to look them up in a book. It's one area where things change so fast, they're out of date by the time they appear in print.

EARTHCAM

http://www.earthcam.com This directory of Web cams provides links to live views of famous city scenes such as the New York skyline and London's Houses of Parliament—as well as interesting sites in categories such as Business and Science.

CAMVISTA

http://www.camvista.com This collection of Web cams focuses on European sites—so it's a great place to check out the scenery in Scotland or Ireland.

DISCOVERY CAMS

http://dsc.discovery.com/cams/cams.html Fancy watching sharks swimming around a giant aquarium, or baby gorillas or polar bears? The Discovery Channel provides a RealVideo feed of what you want—along with other still-picture cams of skyscrapers and even the sun.

Web cams let you see polar bears at the Toledo Zoo or a view of San Francisco's Bay Area.

playing games

**King me. Hit me.
I fold. Go fish.**

Many people buy their computers as an alternative to their Nintendo set. In addition to being a great business tool, communications expert and personal organizer, a computer is a cool games machine. And you don't even need to drive to the mall to buy games to play either—the Web has its own cache of pastimes, most of which are completely free.

Feel like playing a solo game of cards or mah-jongg, or perhaps doing a crossword or word search? You can find sites aplenty that will let you. Two that spring to mind are Microsoft's The Zone (**www.zone.com**) and Yahoo Games (**games.yahoo.com**). Both have more than a hundred free or free-trial games that range from checkers and chess to wilder offerings like Monster Truck Madness and fantasy soccer leagues. Others, including iWin (**www.iwin.com**) and Pogo (**www.pogo.com**) add games of chance like bingo and lotteries to the mix.

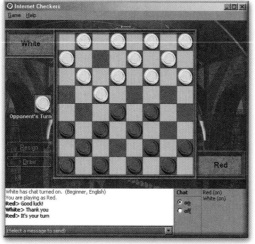

To play, you'll usually have to register at the site—which in the case of Yahoo Games involves making up a user name and giving yourself a password—and log in. Click on a link to visit the game of your choice, and you'll be taken to a special Web page. Expect pages to take a while to open—the games need to be brought across the Internet from the Web site to your computer and then launched, and the games can be quite large programs.

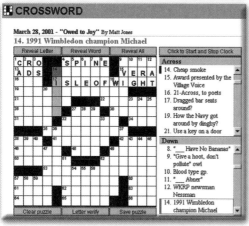

Whether you want to face off against an anonymous foe at the noble sport of checkers, or pit your wits against a crossword, the Web has some sites for you. Microsoft's The Zone (checkers) and Yahoo Games (crossword) are among them.

ASK THE EXPERTS

I want to face off against a real opponent, not a computer. How do I?

There are plenty of opponents waiting in the wings at game sites such as The Zone (**www.zone.com**) and Yahoo Games (**games.yahoo.com**). First, you need to log on to the site, then pick your game—chess, checkers, backgammon or whatever. You'll pick your level—beginner, intermediate or advanced—and then wait for an opponent. You can increase your chances of getting an opponent fast by checking the numbers next to the links you click for the game and level—the larger the number, the more popular the game is at the time. When an opponent at your level checks in, you're automatically connected. But although you're dealing with a live person, game rooms don't usually allow real chat between the two of you. You'll be able to select prewritten messages ("Good luck," "Your move," and so on)—and that's about it. But after all, the play's the thing, not the words.

FIRST PERSON DISASTER STORY

The inside scoop

I'm a big fan of a few of the trickier CD-ROM games. I started in on one the other night and I just couldn't figure it out. I thought maybe there was a programming error and called the company and when I finally got through they said no, my CD-ROM was perfectly fine. And no, they wouldn't tell me how to get to level 3. Hours later, I still hadn't cracked it. I was really annoyed. The next day, I talked to my nephew who is an avid gamesman and he suggested I try **www.gocheat.com**. It's a Web site that provides short cuts and tips to some of the harder computer games out there. I am now back in business and having a blast.

James L., Peoria, Illinois

now what do I do?

Answers to common questions

Some sites I visit contain links to interesting reading material, but I can't open the pages. They use something called Acrobat. What's that?

Acrobat is a technology by Adobe Systems that's been around since before the Web was born, and it's extremely popular online. Basically, an Acrobat document is an exact replica of a printed page; you can't edit it or change it, and it looks exactly the same as a document. That's why the government uses Acrobat documents to make their tax forms available on the Web, and why companies like to use it for their marketing material. Acrobat files (also called PDF or portable document format) need a special program so you can see them. It's called the Acrobat Reader, and you can download it free from Adobe's Web site at **www.adobe.com**. Follow the links for Acrobat at the site.

A friend sent me an MP3 file over e-mail, and it sounded terrible—like AM radio from a weak transmitter. What's up with that?

Don't let this experience sour you on MP3 in general. The fact is that MP3 is a highly compressed format—and you can make the files really small by turning the compression factor up high. When you do this, though, you lose sound quality. It sounds as though your friend really crunched this file down small so it would be easy to send via e-mail, and compromised the sound quality in the process. You can't fix the sound quality on a highly compressed file. Think of it as a recording made on an old cassette tape on a cheap tape deck—it's always going to sound inferior. On a side note, it's bad form to distribute copyrighted music via e-mail. I hope this was something your buddy had permission to distribute.

Why do I keep getting error messages when I visit video Web sites?

Probably because they are very busy sites. Whenever a Web server gets too busy for the traffic, it throws up its hands (virtually) and says, "I can't help you right now!" Just hit the Refresh or Reload button after a second or two, and you'll get what you want.

I paid $2 to download the Liquid Audio file of a Madonna song to my PC, but I can't get it to play on my computer. Why not?

Because computer music files have such good sound quality, record companies are afraid that they will be used for pirating music. They build in all kinds of copy-protection schemes to prevent people from, in their eyes, stealing music. Liquid Audio provides an authorization, called a passport, to copy files between computers. These passports are free and are automatically assigned after you've filled out a passport application at the Liquid Audio site. Sounds as though you have a glitch in your passport. Reapply for one and provide information such as your credit card number, address and phone number. You won't get billed or get bombarded with telemarketing phone calls, but they want this information anyway.

Can I get radio broadcasts online? Yes.

The one plug-in software that you'll need is RealNetworks RealPlayer, which you can download from **www.real.com**. It might already be on your hard disk. Then, you can tune in to any of the following stations for an audio fix as you work:

http://radio.broadcast.com
http://www.liveconcerts.com
http://www.radiofreeworld.com

 **N**OW WHERE DO I GO?!

CONTACTS	PUBLICATIONS
The Internet Movie Database **www.imdb.com** There are no movies to watch here, but IMDB is the most fascinating reference for movie lovers and avid film students alike.	**MP3 Underground** By Ron White and Michael White **300 Incredible Things for Game Players on the Internet** By Charlyn Chisholm
CNET Music **http://music.cnet.com** Once you're familiar with MP3s, this guide helps you locate, organize, and arrange your online music collections with product reviews, how-to articles and other resources.	

CHAPTER 10 CHATTING ONLINE

YOU DON'T NEED A PHONE TO REACH OUT AND
TOUCH SOMEONE. ALL YOU REALLY NEED IS A
KEYBOARD, A COMPUTER AND THE INTERNET.
WHEN YOU'RE THERE, YOU CAN CHAT WITH
DOZENS OF PEOPLE—WITH NARY A BUSY
SIGNAL TO BE HEARD. IMAGINE!

CHATTING ONLINE

what is chatting?

Let your fingers do the talking

Online chat is a typed conversation in the here and now. That means you can only chat with people who are online at the same time as you are (and who share the same chat software—more on that later). Unlike e-mail, there's no time lag with chat. You type a message, and within seconds you get an answer—which is why one-on-one chat is often called **instant messaging** or IM for short.

Instant messages are the easiest type of online chat. If you're a subscriber to America Online or CompuServe, you're already fixed up with the right software to chat with anyone who's online at the time. It's no substitute for physically getting together—people in online chats recognize this when they talk about meeting "in real life" as opposed to online—but online chatting is a fascinating culture that lets you experience the world of the Internet as never before.

STEP BY STEP: HOW CHATTING WORKS

1

What's online chat like, you ask? Well, once your chat software is running, it shapes up pretty much like this.

1. A friend types your user name into the address field and a greeting into the chat message area and clicks on the Send icon.

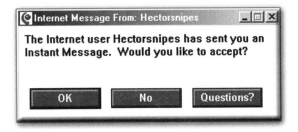

2. You then get a notification that someone wants a chat, and you see the name of that someone. If you don't know the person or want to give him the silent treatment, you can click on No. Otherwise, click on OK.

2

3. You'll then see the greeting. If you want to reply, you click on the Respond button. This opens up a little word-processing box underneath the screen where you can enter your reply. When the reply's all written, click on the Send button.

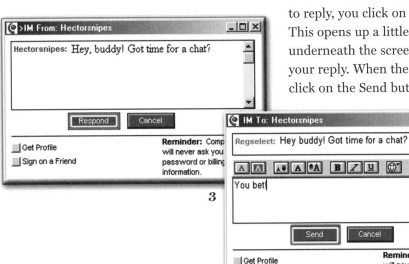

3

4

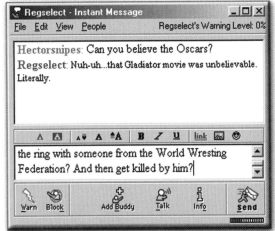

4. Your **chat buddy** (that's the technical term for your friend, by the way) will get your response, type another, and click on send . . . and you'll carry on in this way for as long as you want to chat.

Does this sound like fun or even a useful way to spend your time online? Then turn the page and read on to see how to set up your computer for instant messaging.

getting set for chat

Instant messages . . . Before you can chat, you need special chat software. It isn't difficult to install or use. The good news is that if you subscribe to America Online, CompuServe or Earthlink, you already have chat software called **Instant Messenger.** Subscribers to MSN and most Windows 95 and Internet Explorer users have different chat software called **MSN Messenger**. These programs are set to run whenever you're online.

To send someone an instant message, you need to know two things: their **screen name** (the name they use when chatting—it can be the same as the first part of their e-mail name, no @ or .com needed), and whether they are online or not. Click on the Send Message button and a chat window will appear. Type in the screen name of your buddy, followed by a message, and your chat's ready to begin. Of course, if your friend is not online at the time you type the mes-

sage, you won't get any response; in that case, you might as well send a regular e-mail. That's why online chat software lets you create a list of your favorite people who share the same chat software as you. When you log on, it will tell you who is online from your list. If your first buddy is not online, go down your list until you find someone who is, and then you can chat.

SK THE EXPERTS

I don't have chat software on my computer.
What can I do?

Chat programs are free to download, install and use. So first, find out which software the people you want to chat with use—such as Microsoft's MSN Messenger or AOL's Instant Messaging, also known as AIM. Then go to Download.com and in the Search box enter the name of whichever chat software program you want. You don't have to be a subscriber to AOL or Microsoft's MSN to download their software. The result of the search will be a download link for the chat software. Click to download and install. Bingo! You're ready to chat.

My friends use MSN Messenger and they can't chat with me on America Online. What can I do?

MSN Messenger uses a different chat network from America Online, but you can still chat with MSN people by downloading MSN software and running it when you go online. You can run two types of chat software at a time.

How do I add names to my buddy list?

To add names to the list, click on your software's List Setup tab and click on the New Name entry. Enter as many screen names as you like, and the software will add them to your list. When you click back to the Online tab, you'll see a list of all those people who are online.

chat rooms

Do you come here often?

Unlike instant messaging, **chat rooms** (sites on the Internet devoted to chatting) don't require special software. Your browser will be enough. In America Online, CompuServe and other online services, there's a big button labeled People that you can click on to find communities of people. If you use another Internet service provider, you're still in luck. Pick any Web directory—Yahoo, Google, Excite, and so on—and click through its Internet links until you find Chat. There, you'll see rooms divided by interest (movies, music styles, and so on). Click on one that looks interesting, and you'll be whisked off to the site.

Chat rooms can be bewildering at first sight—lots of lines of text scrolling by and announcements about people entering the room and leaving it. So just sit back and watch a while before you type a message. You'll soon see a pattern emerge of conversations going on between different members in the room—sometimes several at once. If you see a conversation you like, jump in with a comment, but address it to one person so they know you're talking to them.

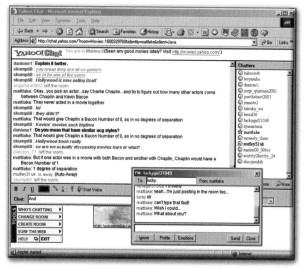

In a chatroom, you see a lot of text flash by quickly, but it doesn't take long to find out who's having the good conversations. And it's easy to join in. You can even talk privately to individuals in the room (see the inset instant message box).

ASK THE EXPERTS

On my first visit to a chat room, someone sent me an instant message. How can I do the same?

If you're chatting with someone and the "**noise**" (amount or quality of typed conversation) in the room gets too much, it's easy to take your chat into one-on-one instant messaging. Just click or double-click on the name of your chat friend, and an instant message window will pop up. Type in your message and click the Send button, and you're away. Just remember that some people will be typing to the room at the same time, so there may be long gaps between your greeting and any reply.

FIRST PERSON DISASTER STORY

No chatting on the job

I was having a great time in a chat room about movies. People were talking about their Oscar picks, and making lots of witty comments about actors. I got on particularly well with one person, who sent me an instant message. We had a nice private chat too, and I thought everything was going well. When it was time to log off, he asked me for my e-mail address, and I gave him my work e-mail. Boy, was that a mistake. My chat buddy (who turns out to be a great guy) sent me quite a few messages, which I replied to during the course of the work day. He forwarded me some jokes he'd got via e-mail. It turns out my company has a program that screens e-mail messages for "inappropriate" content. My boss took me aside and told me to knock off the personal e-mail. Yikes! Now I only give out my personal e-mail address to chat buddies, and not my work one.

Melinda F., Albuquerque, New Mexico

chat etiquette

It sounds like a quaint notion in the high-tech world, but etiquette is alive and well online. Whenever you throw a bunch of people together without knowing their age, gender and cultural background . . . well, there are bound to be misunderstandings. And that's why most chat sites provide certain ground rules.

The code of conduct varies from site to site, so it always pays to check on the rules at any site you visit. But in general, chat etiquette boils down to the following guidelines.

1. Look before you leap. When you first enter a chat room, hold back until you get a feel for the mood of the place. Some people may say "hi" right away, so say "hi" back, but don't launch into a diatribe until you get a feel for the way the conversation's going. And if you think it's too dull or too outspoken, just leave without a word and find somewhere you like better.

2. Use the name of the person you're writing to. This isn't just a Dale Carnegie-style gimmick for winning friends and influencing people. In a fast-moving chat session, people may not realize you're talking to them. So start each line you type with the name of the intended recipient.

3. Reply to people who address you. Unless someone's being deliberately unpleasant in their messages, everyone deserves a reply. Be courteous, be brief if you've nothing to say, but acknowledge what people say to you.

4. Be courteous by ignoring discourtesy. Common courtesy, it turns out, isn't that common. So if you take the high road, it makes a big difference. If someone makes a crass or unpleasant remark that you don't like, ignore it. Boorish chatters who don't get a rise soon go away.

5. Don't be afraid to ask questions. Most people like to fill in newcomers with the information about ongoing conversations. It can be an excellent way to rejuvenate a lull in the conversation too.

6. Be on your best behavior. Nobody in a new chat room knows who you are, but that's not an excuse to let it all hang out. Chat isn't private, and you're not anonymous when you're in a chat room. If someone complains about your behavior in a chat room, the chat hosts keep a record for a while of what's been typed there, and they can track down any miscreants from their log-in records. This level of big-brother intervention is rare, but it's actually nice to know that nuisances can be weeded out if necessary.

7. DON'T LEAVE YOUR CAPS LOCK ON. Messages written entirely in capital letters are difficult to read, and in chat rooms they are considered the same as shouting. You may want to raise your voice for effect once in a while, but keep it brief.

8. Be sensitive about e-mail requests. Some people are reluctant to give out their e-mail addresses—they may be cautious about getting unwanted messages. But it's okay to ask for or offer an e-mail address with someone you've enjoyed chatting with in a room. Just remember: Don't take it personally if someone won't give out an e-mail address. It's not an insult; it's a preference.

9. Don't give out personal information. No matter how nice somebody may seem to be, you have to be very cautious about giving out any information that might identify you to a fellow chatter. It's not that people online are scarier than other people in real life, it's just that it's harder to size up someone based solely on what they type.

10. Never comment on people's spelling. It's just plain rude—like mocking someone's accent or speech impediment.

chat events

Chat events . . .
the chat show where
you can pose the
questions!

One of the most popular kinds of online chatting is more like a radio call-in show. It's called a **chat event**. America Online, CompuServe, and Web sites like Yahoo and Excite schedule regular chat events that you tune in to at a particular time and date. You've probably seen ads for them at Yahoo, Excite, and other Web sites. Chat events usually revolve around a celebrity or an expert on a hot news topic.

Chat events are staged, meaning there are moderators who screen messages. It's just like a radio or TV phone-in show where a producer screens calls and decides whether to air them or not; but instead of phone calls, online moderators screen typed messages. This can be slow going. To keep things lively, most chat events have chat rooms where attendees can log in while the event is happening, and chat among themselves. These work more like regular chat rooms, with bantering and sentence fragments and general chaos.

Although these two screens show the same chat event (on Yahoo, below, and its junior counterpart, Yahooligans, opposite page), Yahoo has a listing of attendees that you can chat with while the main event is going on. This is like whispering comments about a show as it's going on—and it can help speed things along during a slow reply.

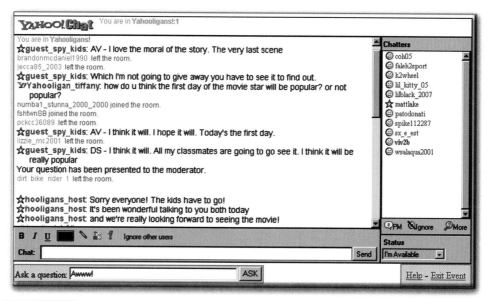

ASK THE EXPERTS

Where can I find out about chat events?

They are listed at most chat sites, and publicized well in advance. Go to any Web directory and follow links to subject areas that interest you, or check in at the chat channels at America Online and other general interest sites. Make a note of the time a chat starts—and especially of the time zone on the schedule! These are live events, not like television shows that are repeated throughout the evening to match prime-time viewing in each zone.

Rats! I logged in half an hour late. How can I find out what I missed?

You're out of luck until the event is over. But within a day, a transcript of most events will be posted on the Web site that hosted the event. Check back at the site later and read over the whole event.

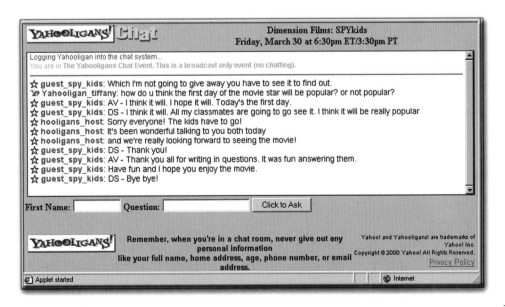

now what do I do?

Answers to common questions

How about explaining some of the cryptic letters I see in chat rooms?

Here's a sampling.

AFK Away From Keyboard, meaning the chatter is stepping out for a while.	**IMHO** In My Humble Opinion, usually sarcastic. There's also IMO (In My Opinion).
BAK Back At Keyboard, the other side of AFK.	**IRL** In Real Life, referring to the life you lead when you're not online.
BBS Usually Be Back Soon, a sign that the chatter will not be away too long.	**JK** Just Kidding.
BRB Be Right Back, same as above.	**LOL** Laughing Out Loud.
BBIA A whole series of acronyms start this way, Be Back In A . . . .BBIAB is "in a bit," BBIAF is "in a few," and in the same context, S and M stand for "second" and "minute."	**NM** Never Mind.
	OTOH On The Other Hand.
CYA Shorthand for "see ya."	**TTYL** Talk To You Later.
GMTA Great Minds Think Alike, and variations abound, including SMTA (Simple Minds Think Alike).	**WB** Welcome Back.
	WTG Way To Go.

How can I stop people from disturbing me with instant messages when I'm busy?

Tell them you're busy! A polite "can't talk right now" is accepted as a matter of courtesy. Of course, you can hang a "do not disturb" sign on your virtual door handle too. In AOL or CompuServe, click on the Status button, select I Am Away, and click OK. In AIM, select MyAIM, Away Message, and select Default Away Message.

I'm being hassled with instant messages from a weird guy I met in a chat room. What can I do?

You can stop him in two ways. First, warn him that he's out of line—some people don't get it and need to be told. If that doesn't stop him, escalate your response. Most instant messenger software lets you block people you don't want to talk to, ever. Next time this guy tries to send an instant message, don't click OK or No, instead check for the Block button and click that. If you don't want to wait around for the next call, add the offender's name to your buddy list, right-click on it, and select Block Buddy. From there on out, your name will be invisible to the offender whenever you're online or not. Unless he knows your e-mail address, there is no way he can contact you.

The sounds from AOL Instant Messenger get on my nerves. How can I turn them off?

It's easy. Click on the My AIM menu, then on Edit Preferences. When the Edit Preferences dialogue box appears, click on the Sounds tab, and click to remove check marks from all the options. When you're done, click on the OK button, and the rest is silence.

OW WHERE DO I GO?!

CONTACTS	PUBLICATIONS
About Chat **http://chatting.about.com/internet/ chatting/** A thorough guide to all things chat—from beginner's advice to lists of great chat rooms.	**It Takes Two.Com** By Kenneth J. Appel
	Complete Idiot's Guide to Online Dating and Relating By Joe Schwartz
Chat.com **www.chat.com** An intermediate-level site from CNET that provides links to all kinds of chat resources.	**Cyberflirt : How to Attract Anyone, Anywhere on the World Wide Web** By Susan Rabin and Barbara Lagowski

CHAPTER 11 KIDS AND THE INTERNET

AS CHILDREN GROW, THEY HAVE AN INSATIABLE APPETITE FOR THE NEW AND INTERESTING. AND THAT'S EXACTLY WHAT THE WEB CAN PROVIDE. HERE'S A CHILD-FRIENDLY GUIDE THAT LEAVES OUT THE JUNK FOOD AND SERVES UP A PLATTER OF THE BEST ONLINE GOODIES.

KIDS AND THE INTERNET

kids online

It's a school!
It's a playground!
It's a TV on steroids!
No, it's . . .
the Internet!

Once children get used to handling a mouse and clicking their way through all those computer software games, the Internet becomes the ultimate cool place to be. It provides a great opportunity for active, hands-on learning and a lot of fun in the process. Like television, the Internet can be habit-forming, and so it's a good idea to set time limits. Also, like television, it contains some stuff you don't want children to see.

But for every downside, there are hundreds of advantages to the Net. So establish a few ground rules and take a couple of precautions so your children can enjoy the biggest adventure playground and learning center in the known universe.

First, consider the ages of your children. Most Internet experts agree that children should be in fourth grade (or 10 years old) before they can surf approved sites on the Net without supervision. That said, if you select the sites and stay around while your children are on them, even a first-grader can benefit from a little online time.

Second, set time limits. Half an hour at a stretch is a good starting time, but figure out what's most comfortable for you. This will pay off later, when you want to take your own turn on the computer and you can't kick your kids off!

Third, do your homework. Check out the sites that kids will like, and educate yourself on how to steer them away from the seamier side of the Net by using filters (see page 186).

Fourth, sit in on as many online sessions with them as you can. This will not only enable you to steer your child to sites you may think they'll enjoy, it will also make the experience more enjoyable.

Fifth, set up an online contract with your kids. To make sure kids commit to your online rules about time and designated sites to hit, write up the rules and make the kids sign an agreement. It makes them realize how important the rules are, which adds to the excitement of going online for the first time.

ASK THE EXPERTS

Using the Internet involves knowing how to type. How old should children be before they learn to type?

Basic keyboard skills are a good exercise for any child who can read, and CD-ROM games that encourage little children to type in their names before they play are a good way to start. But learning to **touch type** (type without looking at the keyboard) is more appropriate for children seven or more years old. If your second- and third-graders aren't learning typing at school, buy a typing software program for your home computer. There are three programs to choose from: Mavis Beacon Teaches Typing (**www.mavisbeacon.com**), Typing Tutor (**www.knowledgeadventure.com**) and Typing Instructor (**www.individualsoftware.com**).

I am concerned about my children using the Internet. Where can I go for more information?

One of the best sources is SafeKids (**www.safekids.com**), a site that manages to be really upbeat and positive without being a Pollyanna. It provides great advice for parents and children, including an online safety contract that parents and children can agree to. For the parents, there's well-thought-out advice for online family use; and for the children, there's some neat audio—including someone going through online safety rules, and a safety song sung by Daffy Dave. Don't be overly concerned about Internet safety. It's a lot like teaching your children other rules about safety, such as not opening the door to strangers, and not getting into cars with people they don't know.

sites just for kids

What are your kids interested in?

The problem with the Web for kids is that there's just too much of it. No matter what your progeny likes, there will be dozens of sites devoted to it. One of the best ways to find the good stuff is to check out so-called **portal sites**, big sites that list the cool stuff at other Web sites. Here's a sampling of some of the top young people's portals.

MSN Kids
http://kids.msn.com
Neatly divided into under-nine and over-nine groups (for that all-important crossover into third grade), MSN's children's sites are a great collection of links to activities, articles, jokes, news, games and fun educational sites across the Web. It's not strong in searching for other sites (as Yahooligans is), but it's a decent enough starting place.

The ALA's 700+ amazing sites
http://www.ala.org/parentspage/greatsites
The American Library Association web site has a great collection of information for parents, but its biggest draw is a current list of more than 700+ great sites for children to visit, broken down into broad categories of Arts and Entertainment, Literature and Language, People Past and Present, Planet Earth and Beyond, and Science and Technology. Like all libraries, the ALA's site includes a nice mixture of educational and entertaining material.

Yahooligans
http://www.yahooligans.com
Think of Yahoo devoted to kids' sites. That's what Yahoo did—and the result was Yahooligans. It's a directory of kid-friendly sites across the Web, all listed in subject areas such as Arts & Entertainment, Science & Nature, and Sports—with a search engine that can root out sites of special interest in one step. Better yet, the site includes lots of special content, such as kid-oriented news and chat events.

Ask Jeeves for Kids
http://www.ajkids.com

AskJeeves is the friendliest of the search sites. Not only is it hosted by a cartoon character, it handles questions in a kid-friendly way. You type in a real-language question (such as, "Why is the sky blue?" or "What makes waves?"), and click on the Ask button. AskJeeves serves up a series of relevant questions and answers. If one of the answers is the one you're looking for, you click on it, and you're whisked off to the site.

Education.com's KidSpace
http://www.education.com/kidspace/

There's plenty of free-access stuff at KidSpace, but at this site you have to sign up as a member to get to the good stuff. But don't let this bother you—there are special sign-up screens for under-12s, teens and adults that ensure that your kids aren't probed for information you don't want them to give out. You do have to provide a parental e-mail address for the site's benefit, but this is for good reasons (which the site explains carefully). And having logged on, your kids (and you) get access to an excellent magazine site, chat, message boards and more.

games for children

Kick a ball, deal cards, or king yourself at checkers . . . with your mouse

Playing is a child's work, they say, and it's a saying that holds especially true on the Web. Almost every site for children has some kind of games included—whether they're educational wordplay, picture-laden arcade-style games, or a reworking of an old classic such as checkers. As children find sites they like, they'll stumble across games they want to play there. Children can click onto the VeggieTales site at **www.bigidea.com** and find themselves facing a pattern-matching arcade game that works a lot like the classic Tetris. Lego buffs will be playing soccer with 3-D images of Lego people. And Harry Potter fans may find themselves almost accidentally in training for the Quidditch season just by clicking around their favorite boy wizard's site.

As with grown-up game sites, kids' games require special programs to make them go. Sometimes they are programs written in a language your browser knows called Java or Javascript. Sometimes they are written in a language such as Shockwave that requires a special (and free) **plug-in program** that enhances your browser. (See pages 152-153 for more on plug-ins.)

Here are a few good sites to find games.

Kid's Domain Games
http://www.kidsdomain.com/games/
Whether your four-year-old is looking to find the Rainbow Fish under one of three shells or a preteen wants to sharpen word skills, Kid's Domain games links will show the way. This site contains links to games at sites all across the Web—sites as varied as Disney, Lego and VeggieTales.

Yahooligans Games
Games.yahooligans.com

Tic-tac-toe, checkers, go fish, spades and a whole lot more child-friendly games are available at the click of a mouse on the Yahooligans' site.

Headbone Zone
www.headbone.com

Headbone Interactive started life as a CD-ROM game manufacturer, but they made the transition to being a hip kid site after a couple of years. They provide some interesting games for older preteens and teens.

Lego Mania
www.lego.com

Whether your children's interests run to soccer or space aliens, there's an animated arcade game at the Lego site to suit their taste.

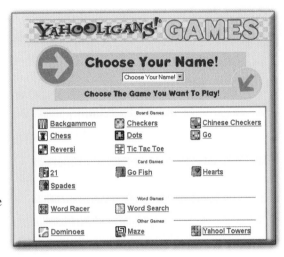

all about filters

Keeping unwanted sites and chat at bay

Chances are, after kicking around on the Internet for a while, you have stumbled upon some "inappropriate" sites. The thought of your kids finding such sites can understandably make you nervous. That's why there's Internet **filtering software,** which was designed to keep children out of adult sites. You set the limits in your filtering software—so that if you don't mind bad language but object to violence, you can set one high, the other low

Filtering software does its filtering in two ways. First, it keeps a list of sites that a panel of Internet reviewers has deemed inappropriate. The software also maintains a word list of George Carlin–style words that you can't say on network television, and checks incoming pages for those words. If they're present, the software blocks the page from loading. (Unfortunately, it will also block out useful sites—for example, medical sites that deal with HIV protection.) Some filtering software also sets time limits on use. Doesn't that make you feel more secure?

Filtering software is built into America Online and CompuServe's software—it's called Parental Controls there. Or you can download any number of filter programs, such as CYBERsitter, Cyber Patrol, Net Nanny and SurfWatch. In each case, you download and install the programs, and then type in the settings that enable you to exclude various inappropriate sites from your kids' surfing habits.

FILTERING SOFTWARE

Here's a list of filtering software you can download and buy to block sites you don't want your kids getting to.

CYBERsitter
http://www.cybersitter.com/

Cyber Patrol
http://www.cyberpatrol.com/

Net Nanny
www.netnanny.com

SurfWatch
http://www.surfwatch.com/

SafeSurf
www.safesurf.com

ASK THE EXPERTS

**Are there any content ratings for Internet sites—
as there are for the movies?**

There is an Internet rating system in place, but it doesn't work like movie or TV ratings. The Internet Content Rating Association **(www.icra.org)** has an optional system adopted by some sites—including many kids' sites and responsible publishers of adult material who want to remain family-friendly. These sites add ratings of their pages for language, sexual content, violence, and substance abuse. Filtering software can check these settings and make sure that content you find objectionable won't come through. But not every site uses this rating system, so unless you set your filtering software to block anything that's not rated, objectionable stuff may get through. And if you do set the maximum rating, you'll block off all kinds of good stuff too. It's a trade-off that you have to decide for yourself.

FIRST PERSON   DISASTER STORY

How I turned into an Internet snoop

I was getting increasingly worried about the time my daughter spent on her computer. What was she doing? One day I turned on her computer to check it out. I knew I could see the sites she'd been visiting by looking into her browser History list. My daughter visited HotMail a lot, so I poked around the papers on her desk and found her password. Every week or so, I'd check her e-mail messages. Mostly it was just messages from her school friends, and occasionally a forwarded list of teenage jokes—nothing to worry about. The trouble is, my daughter figured out that someone was visiting HotMail on her computer while she was at school (it notes the times) and confronted me. We had a huge argument about it—just like the one I had with my mother when I found that she'd been reading my diary. I called my mom about it and she remembered our fight and how bad she felt about snooping. She was worried about me "growing up too fast." Just like I was about my daughter! After much talk, and a solemn promise from me not to spy, my daughter forgave me enough to chat with me online (naturally) about personal stuff again, thank goodness.

Natasha K., Portland, Oregon

homework help

"DAAAAD! What's the capital of Pennsylvania?" "I don't know, dear . . . ask your computer."

Your fourth-grader has to write a report on one of the fifty states, including photographs of the state bird and the census figures. Meanwhile, your high-flying high-school junior has to find out the atomic number and weight of the element Tungsten—and, to get extra credit, figure out why its symbol on the periodic table is W.

Will you help them? Heck, no. It's their assignments, so it's their responsibility (and besides which, you have no clue either). So fire up the computer and have your kids surf away at a few choice sites. Directories like Yahoo and Google and Excite are great for finding general information. Encyclopedias like Encarta and Encyclopedia.com are just like their counterparts in print—but with pictures you can copy and use in your reports (with acknowledgments, of course, to appease the copyright gods). And sites like OneLook and Thesaurus are great for looking up words for definitions and alternatives.

But the majority of school-age kids will get more benefit from tools designed for their own ages. KidsClick (**www.kidsclick.org**) and AskJeeves Study Tools (**www.ajkids.com/studytools**), for example, provide some mighty research aids for children. Both include links to pages full of almanac, atlas, dictionary and other handy research information. And of course they also handle Web searching in a kid-friendly way, since both sites are maintained by education librarians.

Assuming that your kids haven't left their assignments to the last minute (hey, we know that's quite an assumption), it might be worth having them contact an expert in a particular subject. Yahooligans lists a collection of sites that have experts in various fields who either answer e-mail messages or post replies to common questions online. To find these sites, check out the box on the next page.

# ASK THE EXPERTS

My fourth-grader is being encouraged to keep up on current events. Where can I find a news service that's not, well, too grown-up?

The Weekly Reader provides a daily news story at **http://www.weeklyreader.com/features/hpress.html** and a weekly digest at **http://www.weeklyreader.com/features/thisweek.html**.

My son's having real trouble at school learning Spanish. How can I "top up" his skills?

Foreign languages are tough for some kids. As a general rule, it's the stuff that kids learn on their own that sticks best. So visit one of the sites that provides occasional free lessons in the language—such as TravLang (**www.travlang.com**) and LingoLex (**www.lingolex.com/spanish.htm**). Both of these sites ease kids into Spanish through practice and lessons—though TravLang handles lots of other languages too and has a high-powered course that you have to subscribe to.

My son loves reading magazines, but I can't get him interested in browsing the Web for his homework research.

Try enticing him online with a magazine site. Weekly Reader Galaxy is a good starting point (**http://www.weeklyreader.com**), with its features, polls, and daily updates.

ONLINE STUDY AIDS

KidsClick
www.kidsclick.org

Study Tools
http://www.ajkids.com/studytools/

FactMonster
www.factmonster.com

Yahooligans School Bell
http://www.yahooligans.com/School_Bell (click on Ask an Expert for more help)

kids e-mailing

Welcome to the world of e-pals

Once upon a time, finding pen pals required a lot of interaction between school administrations in different countries, and it was often a hassle. Nowadays, youngsters can find e-pals just by joining Web sites. And they can exchange e-mail messages with their real-life buddies too.

Ah, but how old should a child be before getting an e-mail address? It depends. Many teachers and parents feel okay about letting eleven-year-olds have their own accounts. Others hold off until the child reaches teen age. A lot depends on your children, of course.

Can they be trusted not to give out personal information, such as their real name, home address and phone number? If they are responsible, then consider getting them a free Web e-mail account at such sites as the Headbone Zone, ePALS, and KidSpace Connection.

Sit with your child when signing him or her up at these sites. Often these sites ask for an adult's e-mail address for verification, which you can provide. Ask your child to come up with an e-mail name that is not too revealing, such as a nickname or a funny made-up name—anything but their real name.

After that, the mailbox belongs to the child, and as long as parents don't interfere, the kids will get used to the process at their own pace. They'll pass out their e-mail address to friends. When they visit kids' chat sites, they'll hand it out to people they meet there. And the communication will begin.

ASK THE EXPERTS

I don't want my kids exposed to any e-mail messages from strangers. What can I do?

Tell kids to be very careful about who they give their e-mail address to. They shouldn't give it out on sweepstakes or other paper-based applications forms, because this invariably leads to the information being used for direct marketing. They shouldn't post it on message forums or news groups designed for grown-ups, because then grown-ups may begin to send messages directly to them, taking issue with their postings.

I overheard my daughter on the phone, saying she gets e-mail from people she doesn't know. It bothers me, but I don't know how to bring it up.

The most important thing is to let your children know that if unwanted e-mail shows up, they should let you know about it. Don't push them to show any e-mail, though—they'll either be willing to share it or not. Tell them that they can forward e-mail messages to you if they're not sure what to do about them. And here's the most important thing: Even if it's something you find offensive, don't make a federal incident out of it—that'll just discourage your kids from being open with you in future. Offer to deal with it, then check out all the filtering options with the company that provides the e-mail account. It should be easy to block messages from senders—and the e-mail provider will be able to show you how.

I don't want to pry in my children's e-mail boxes, but I do wonder what they're up to.

Then don't pry. It's not worth losing your children's trust by opening their e-mail. Did your parents steam open your paper mail when you were young? They didn't? Then don't start a new family tradition! If you feel as though you must look at your children's e-mail messages, then you're not ready to let them have e-mail accounts yet.

WEB E-MAIL AND COMMUNITIES FOR KIDS

Want to get an e-mail address for your kids to hand out? Look no further than these sources. Like grown-up Web e-mail sites, these will provide places for kids to send and receive messages. Unlike adult e-mail sites, most of them filter out messages to ensure that offensive "spam" won't find its way into the Inbox.

ePALS
www.epals.com

KidLink
www.kidlink.org

Kids' Space Connection Pen Pals
http://www.ks-connection.org/penpal/pen-pal.html

Headbone Zone E-Pals
www.headbone.com

kids and chat

. . . and she was all
like, y'know,
and I was all like . . .
well, sure . . .

Want to know the best typing practice your kids can get? It's replacing the constant hum of teen conversation with the clatter of chat room messaging. Youngsters, as we all know, just love to talk with each other.

If you checked out some of the chat rooms for grown-ups we covered earlier in the book, you'll know that some are more like urban bars than youth clubs—where the conversation won't interest younger people anyway. To kick back and have fun, kids prefer to be in the company of their own kind, not a bunch of boring old wrinklies like their parents. So they'll want to check out youth-oriented chat rooms, such as The Kids Room, Kid's Corner, Teen Hang, and Teen Scene—all of which are at Headbone Zone. Although these sites are free-for-all kids' chat, they are **moderated,** which means that there's always a live adult monitoring the conversation and able to intervene if things get out of hand.

To check in, you must first sign your children up at Headbone Zone (**www.headbone.com**), which requires them to enter your e-mail address. Once that's all squared away, they'll have an e-mail address and chat ID at Headbone Zone, and can visit the chat area, which is at **www.headbone.com/hbzchat**. The rooms all have a 25-person capacity and are open from 2:00 pm to 6:00 pm Pacific time. There are several other juvie hangouts online too. KidLink and the KidsCom Graffiti Wall are among them (at **www.kidlink.org** and **www.kidscom.com** respectively). To find more chat rooms, visit Yahooligans, click on Arts and Entertainment, and click on the Chat link there.

Making e-pals in chat rooms or online message centers is cool, but be sure to tell your kids to tell you about whom they have met. It might be nice for you to say "hi" to them online. If your kids want to meet someone they've met online, be sure to have them ask you first, and accompany them to the meeting.

STEP BY STEP: AOL INSTANT MESSENGER FOR THE WHOLE FAMILY

Daughter, both sons, Mom, and Dad all use the same computer? All like to chat online with their buddies? It's possible to create lots of different log-ins using the free AIM program (that's AOL Instant Messenger, to the long-winded). Here's how.

1. Most AOL users have AIM set up to log them straight onto the AIM service. If you don't, go to **www.aim.com** and download it. Once installed, click on the My AIM menu and select Switch User.

2. You'll see the Sign On page. If you're sharing a computer, you'll want to click to remove the check mark from the Auto-login box, and probably the Save Password box too.

3. Click the little down arrow next to the Screen Name box, and click on the New User option.

4. Click on the Sign On—the little picture of a green running man.

5. If you're using an existing AOL screen name, the process is simple—just click on the Use AOL Screen Name button and enter the AOL password for that screen name. If you're creating a new name, click on Register New Screen Name.

6. A Web page will open asking for the new name, passwords, and some personal information. Enter it all and click on the Next button. Unless someone's already taken the screen name you want, you're done.

Internet safety

For all its wonders, there are a few downsides

The same rules for safety that children need to navigate the real world apply in the cyberworld, but with a few twists. Ideally, you should have the family computer in an open area of your house, so it is easily in view. If you do have a computer in a child's room, you can either not connect it up to the Internet until they are at least 10 years old or install filtering software (see page 186).

It's a good idea to tell your children that you will be checking their Internet activity from time to time. To view the sites your child has visited, simply click the History button on the browser and you'll see a list of the most recently visited sites. Also, check any files or programs your children may have downloaded from the Internet. To do that, check the directory that programs are downloaded into. It's also a good idea to look through files you don't recognize.

Monitor your children's use of the computer. The computer is not a baby-sitter; it's a complex tool, full of fun and, alas, mayhem. For that reason, be sure to teach your children to treat strangers they come in contact with on the Internet like real-life strangers. Tell them not to reveal personal information about themselves or their family to cyber-strangers and never agree to meet with them without parental supervision.

Even with these safeguards, unwanted or uncomfortable Internet experiences can occur. Here's how to help your child cope with them. First, explain to your children that if someone or some site online is bothering them or sending them unwanted material, they do not have to respond. Second, if the problem continues, they should tell you. Be careful not to make your children feel somehow at fault for any unwanted online messages; the goal is to stop Internet problems before they get out of hand. How do you stop them? See the following page for specifics.

ASK THE EXPERTS

What do I do if my child gets a hurtful e-mail from someone she knows online?

Children often use the Internet to e-mail their friends. If communication gets out of hand and your children are sent mean e-mail messages, tell them not to reply in kind, because e-mail can come back to haunt you. It's easy to escalate into an e-mail war, which often gets copied and sent to other friends. Best to take the high road.

I think my teenage daughter is being harassed by someone online. What should I do?

You have to handle these issues carefully. You don't want to blow a harmless but annoying issue out of proportion, and you certainly don't want to let a serious problem continue or escalate. First, try to discover the scope of the problem. Ask your daughter to report offensive chat messages to the site that maintains the chat room site. (In chat rooms, the offender can't know who's reporting him. Chat room sessions are usually monitored and archived.) Keep unpleasant e-mail messages as evidence too—they can be used against any harasser. And visit child protection sites such as **www.pedowatch.org** and **www.ncmec.org** for detailed advice on how to proceed.

My son just received an e-mail from an acquaintance threatening school violence. What should he do?

Schools have zero tolerance about threats or even jokes about school violence, but some kids will still act tough by making empty threats or stupid comments about it. Your son's probably reluctant to squeal on a peer, but threats or comments about something this serious put him in an awkward position. If he thinks his acquaintance is being a jerk, he could deflect the issue by writing back: "Don't you know that e-mail and chat sessions can be monitored by the authorities?" is an effective (and true) statement that should do the job. But if there's any hint that the boy in question might be serious, your son should follow up his warning by following the school policy on these matters. It's a tough position for your son to be in, but the responsibility falls squarely on the guy who's stupid enough to make the threats.

now what do I do?

Answers to common questions

You've hardly mentioned any Web sites for kids. Aren't there any more?

Excuse the oversight! There are so many Web sites for children, we could fill many pages with them. You want proof? Here you go!

Web search sites for kids
AskJeeves for Kids
www.ajkids.com

KidsClick
sunsite.berkeley.edu/KidsClick!/

Yahooligans
www.yahooligans.com

Kids' Communities
ePals
www.epals.com

KidLink
www.kidlink.org

Kids' Space Connection Pen Pals
http://www.ks-connection.org/ penpal/penpal.html

Headbone Zone E-Pals
www.headbone.com

Encyclopedias and dictionaries
Encyclopedia.com
www.encyclopedia.com

Encarta
www.encarta.com

Onelook Dictionaries
www.onelook.com

Roget's Internet Thesaurus
www.thesaurus.com

FactMonster
www.factmonster.com

Math and money
Allowance Net
www.allowancenet.com

Ask Dr Math
www.askdrmath.com

CoolMath
www.coolmath.com

Cultural icons
American Girl
www.americangirl.com

Harry Potter
www.harrypotter.com

Nick Jr.
www.nickjr.com

Mary Kate and Ashley Olsen
www.marykateandashley.com

Pokemon World
www.pokemon.com

Zoog Disney
www.zoogdisney.com

Games and pastimes
Headbone Zone
www.headbone.com

Fleetkids
www.fleetkids.com

Making Friends
www.makingfriends.com

Bonus.com
www.bonus.com

Conjuror.com
www.conjuror.com

KidsDomain
www.kidsdomain.com/

Science

Bill Nye The Science Guy
www.billnye.com

Discovery Channel Space pages
www.discovery.com/guides /space/space.html

NASA's Star Child astronomy page
www.nasa.gov/kids.html

Exploratorium
www.exploratorium.com

U.S. Geological Survey Volcano page
Vulcan.wr.usgs.gov

World Wildlife Foundation
www.worldwildlife.org

Silly stuff

Yucky.com
www.yucky.com

Hamster Dance
http://www.hamsterdance2 .com/hampsterdance2.html

Fishy Dance
www.fishydance.com

Languages

TraveLang lessons
(multiple languages)
www.travelang.com

LingoLex Learn Spanish
www.lingolex.com/spanish.htm

French
www.zipzapfrance.com

Babelfish Translation service
babelfish.altavista.com

 **N**OW WHERE DO I GO?!

CONTACTS	PUBLICATIONS
Family PC magazine **www.familypc.com** This monthly magazine and its Web site are devoted to families who use computers. Like most computer magazines, they include many product reviews, but the magazine focuses a lot on using the Internet and computers for constructive family fun.	**The Everything Kids Online Book** by Rich Mintzer & Carole F Mintzer **Jeeves, I Need Help!** by Callie Gregory and Lynda Green **Online Kids** by Preston Gralla
NetMom **http://www.netmom.com/** Written by Jean Armour Polly, the author of The Internet Kids Family Yellow Pages, 4th edition, Netmom is a column that's devoted to kid-friendly and useful Web sites.	

glossary

Active Window Even when you have lots of different windows open, you can only work on one at a time. It's called the active window, and you can tell which it is by looking at the title bar. On the active window, it will be brightly colored, and the others will be fainter.

Address To Internet users, there are two types of addresses—Web page and e-mail. Web page addresses (called URLs) look like this—http://www.bn.com. And e-mail addresses look like this—info@bn.com.

Address Book The online equivalent of a little black book of phone numbers, your e-mail software's address book contains contact names and their e-mail addresses.

BCC (Blind Carbon Copy) An e-mail setting that lets you send a copy of a message to someone secretly—so the other recipients can't see the e-mail address.

Bookmark You can't slip a piece of card between Web pages to keep your place, but your Web browser can keep a record of sites that you want to return to. These records are called Bookmarks—or Favorites, or Favorite Places, depending on your browser.

Browser A program used to view (and hear) the information on the World Wide Web. The most popular are Microsoft Internet Explorer, Netscape Navigator and Netscape Communicator.

Byte A byte is the basic unit of storage on your computer. It's so small that most of the files you'll see are measured in thousands of bytes (kilobytes, or KB) or millions of bytes (megabytes or MB).

CC (Carbon Copy) An e-mail setting that lets you send a copy of a message to more than one e-mail address at once.

Chat On a computer, chat doesn't involve your voice at all. It's a typed conversation between two or more people, all of whom are online at the same time. Chats can take place in chat room sites or by using a program like AOL's Instant Messenger.

Cookie A little text file that many Web sites save on your hard disk, used to help the site recognize you as you move from page to page.

Default A choice made by the software program when you, the user, don't respond. Defaults are built into all software programs to make them easier and faster to use.

Digital Everything that goes on in your computer is digital—it's a code made up of long strings of digits (0s and 1s)—unlike telephone or radio signals, which are made up of lots of different frequencies.

Desktop In Windows, the Desktop is everything you see on the screen before you open any programs or folders. It consists of the My Computer and other icons and any wallpaper pictures you may have.

Dialog Box Any box that appears and asks you to click on a button or enter a word is called a dialog box. It's called that because Windows wants you to respond in some way—like two people talking.

Domain The Internet's address system is based on domains. Where postal addresses have Zip codes and street names, the Internet uses Top Level Domains (TLDs) and domain names. The top level domain is the cluster of letters after the last period in a Web address (.com, .net, .org, .gov, .edu and so on). A domain name consists of a name and the TLD—such as fi.edu or bn.com.

Double-Click When you're asked to double-click on something in Windows, you move the mouse until the cursor is over the object, and you click the left mouse button twice in quick succession.

Download To take a file, Web page, or e-mail message from a computer on the Internet and deliver it to your own computer.

E-Mail Typed messages that are delivered from one computer to another over the Internet.

Extension All Windows files have a file name and a file extension. The extension is up to three characters long and is listed after the file name and a period. Most of the time, you don't even see the file extension—Windows Explorer conceals most of them.

Favorite, Favorite Place See Bookmark.

FAQ Frequently asked questions or FAQs should be your first port of call at a new Web site. They are Web pages that tell you information you need to know about a Web site or the subject the Web site is dedicated to.

File All the information you see on a computer, and all the programs you run, are stored in files.

File Format Because a computer file can contain programs, pictures, text, or sounds, each type of information is stored in a different way. This is called the file format, and it's usually referred to by its "file **extension**." A picture from the Internet may be in GIF or JPEG format, for example.

Flame An angry or insulting piece of e-mail. It's easy to hurt people's feelings in e-mail, so be sure to read over your messages to avoid starting a flame war (angry e-mail exchange).

Folder In Windows, as in a regular office, files are stored in folders. Using Windows Explorer, you'll see little manila folder icons tucked away in most drives. Double-click on them, and they will open up to reveal the files inside.

Format See File Format.

Home Page Home refers to a number of things: 1. the first page you see in when you start your Web browser; 2. the first page you see when you visit a Web site; and 3. Your personal page on the Web.

Host Any computer you can reach on the Internet is called a host.

HTML Hypertext markup language—the code used to write Web pages. It creates text formatting, defines the position of graphics, and creates links to other Web pages.

HTTP Hypertext transfer protocol. The code that browsers use to transfer Web pages appears in the address field of your browser. Sometimes you'll see an s at the end—https://—which shows that the page you're viewing is on a super-secure server.

Hyperlink See Link.

Internet A massive network of computers that stretches across the whole world.

Internet Service Provider (ISP) Any company that can hook you up to the Internet is called an Internet Service Provider. These companies usually provide a phone number for your computer to dial, or provide special customer service.

Link Web pages contain text or graphics that you can click on, and that take you to other Web pages. These are called links—and are often underlined or surrounded with blue lines.

Menu Bar The place at the top of a program where you find menu options like File, Edit and Help.

Modem The gadget that lets your computer talk to computers on the Internet.

MP3 The most popular way to share music on the Internet, MP3 files are like CD singles in a computer file.

Newbie A newcomer to the Internet. It's a mild insult, but you don't have to endure it for long.

Online Service Online services are Internet Service Providers that add special private sites and services that regular Internet users can't get to. America Online, CompuServe and the Microsoft Network are three examples.

Properties Properties sounds more complicated than it really is. Every file and program in Windows has a Properties box. You simply right-click on its icon and select Properties to view it. There you'll see the file's date, size and other details about it.

Right-click There are two or more buttons on a PC's mouse—and when you're asked to right-click, you simply click on the button on the right side.

Search Engine A program that searches for things on the Web—usually the general content of Web pages; but some search engines specialize in videos, sound files or even news stories.

Server Any computer on a network that provides a service is a server. The types of services available on the Internet include e-mail handling, Web data and file transfer.

Service Provider See Internet Service Provider and Online Service.

Spam Also known as bulk e-mail, direct e-mail or just plain junk, spam is the derogatory name given to unwanted e-mail.

Start Button The Start button, at the bottom of your screen, is the rectangle with a little Windows flag that you click on to start programs in Windows, and also to start the Windows shut-down process.

Taskbar The bottom strip that contains the Start button and the icons of programs that are running.

Title Bar The title bar is the top part of a window. At the left, it contains the name and icon of the program, and at the right, three buttons that you use to minimize, maximize or close the window.

Tool Bar A bar with buttons or icons. Used to set graphic functions such as changing fonts and type size.

URL Stands for Uniform Resource Locator, a horribly long-winded way of saying Web address.

Zip File To make computer files quicker to send over the Internet, people compress them into zip files. Before they can use them again, they have to uncompress them—like putting one of those dried-out sponges into water and watching it grow.

index

W

THE AUTHOR: UP CLOSE

Matt Lake has been explaining the inner workings of computers to beginners and experts alike for more than 12 years. He is a former staff editor at *PC World*, *PC/Computing* and CNET—and has written about how to use technology in the real world for such publications as *The New York Times*, *Small Business Computing* and *Computers Made Easy*. But he still hasn't forgotten what it's like to be a beginner—mainly because when he's not writing about computers, he's providing computer support and training at schools, libraries and other nonprofit organizations (including his extended family).

From his home office, Lake uses the Internet to read newspapers, listen to the radio, buy things and discuss things he's interested in. He exchanges e-mail with friends, colleagues and family from the United States and the United Kingdom to Germany, Hungary and New Zealand. "I couldn't possibly keep in touch with all these people if I only had pen and paper to rely on," says Lake.

Barbara J. Morgan Publisher, Silver Lining Books

I'm on the Internet, Now What?! ™

Barb Chintz Editorial Director

Leonard Vigliarolo Design Director

Ann Stewart Picture Research

Della R. Mancuso Production Manager

Marguerite Daniels Editorial Assistant